An Important Message to Our Readers

This product provides information and general advice about the law. But laws and procedures change frequently, and they can be interpreted differently by different people. For specific advice geared to your specific situation, consult an expert. No book, software or other published material is a substitute for personalized advice from a knowledgeable lawyer licensed to practice law in your state.

3rd edition

The Inventor's Notebook

By Fred Grissom & Attorney David Pressman

NOLO

Keep Up-to-Date

To keep its books up-to-date, Nolo issues new printings and new editions periodically. New printings reflect minor legal changes and technical corrections. New editions contain major legal changes, major text additions or major reorganizations. To find out if a later printing or edition of any Nolo book is available, call Nolo at 510-549-1976 or check our website at http://www.nolo.com.

To stay current, follow the "Update" service at our website at http://www.nolo.com/lawstore/update/list.cfm. In another effort to help you use Nolo's latest materials, we offer a 35% discount off the purchase of the new edition of your Nolo book when you turn in the cover of an earlier edition.

Third Edition	
Second Printing	APRIL 2002
Editor	RICHARD STIM
Cover Design	TONI IHARA
Book Design	TERRI HEARSH
Proofreading	ROBERT WELLS
Printing	BERTELSMANN SERVICES, INC.

Grissom, Fred E.
    The inventor's notebook   / by Fred Grissom & David Pressman.--3rd ed.
      p.   cm.
    Includes bibliographical references and index.
    ISBN 0-87337-599-8
    1. Patent laws and legislation--United States--Popular works. 2. Inventions--Popular works. 3. Inventors--United States--Handbooks, manuals, etc. I. Pressman, David 1937–
II. Title.

KF3114.6.G75   2000
346.7304'86--dc21

                                                      00-035675

For information on bulk purchases or corporate premium sales, please contact the Special Sales Department. For academic sales or textbook adoptions, ask for Academic Sales. Call 800-955-4775 or write to Nolo at 950 Parker Street, Berkeley, CA 94710.

Dedication

To our wives—Shelley, for her faith and sense of humor, and Roberta, for her perseverance and style.

Acknowledgments

The authors wish to express their thanks and appreciation to the crew at Nolo, especially Jake Warner, Richard Stim and Steve Elias of Nolo for their invaluable advice and sustaining enthusiasm. We also thank Paul Guyton and David Joyner for stoking the creative fires with their critical insights, and Andromache Warner for her valuable advice on doing market research. And thanks to Terri Hearsh for her thoughtful design of the 3rd edition.

Table of Contents

Introduction

What The Inventor's Notebook Does and How to Use It

1 Using the Notebook

Appendixes

▌ Notebook

▌▌ Worksheets

III Glossary

IV Fee Schedule

V Tear-Out Forms

Consultant's Work Agreement

Proprietary Materials Agreement

Joint Owner's Agreement

Assignment of Invention and Patent Application

Universal License Agreement

Request for Participation in Disclosure Document Program

Invention Disclosure Statement

Provisional Patent Application Cover Letter

What The Inventor's Notebook Does and How to Use It

There are four main activities that all successful inventors must normally undertake:

- conceiving, building, and testing the invention
- legally protecting the invention
- marketing the invention, and
- financing the first three tasks.

The Inventor's Notebook is designed to help you organize the records you need to successfully complete each of these activities. Specifically, *The Inventor's Notebook* will show you how to document the details of your invention in order to:

- maintain good records of your inventing process. By doing this you will always know exactly where you are in the invention process and what remains to be done. This will help you avoid dead ends and the repetition of mistakes;
- create a legal record that you are the first and true inventor. If your invention is ever challenged, your completed notebook will be the foundation of the legal protection for your idea;
- convince others of the worth of your invention;
- proceed realistically in terms of your invention's commercial potential; and
- organize all the information pertaining to your invention in one location.

A. Brief Description of The Inventor's Notebook

The Inventor's Notebook is designed for a single invention. You should use a separate book for each invention. It consists of:

- Chapter 1: Using the Notebook
- Chapter 2: Legal Protection
- Chapter 3: Marketing
- Chapter 4: Financing
- Chapter 5: Help Beyond This Book
- Appendix I: Notebook (bound forms to create a record of your invention)
- Appendix II: Worksheets (forms to help you determine the commercial feasibility of your invention and maintain its confidentiality prior to its receiving a patent)
- Appendix III: Glossary (words which describe the hardware, parts, and function of your invention in specifications and claims)
- Appendix IV: Fee Schedule (as of February 2002)
- Appendix V: Tear-out Forms (agreements for maintaining confidentiality, joint ownership, and licensing inventions; forms for assigning ownership and invention disclosure statements; and cover letter form for provisional patent application).

Each chapter begins with a brief overview of its contents. The sections within each chapter begin with instructions for completing the corresponding forms. We also provide one or two specific references for additional background reading.

In some instances we offer you several copies of a form. This is because, as you know, the inventive process is interactive and commonly gives rise to more than one version of the invention. These versions are usually harmonized before you file your patent application, but until this occurs it is essential that you record the details of each version.

B. Scope of The Inventor's Notebook

The purpose of *The Inventor's Notebook* is to provide you with an organized means for documenting your inventive efforts. We do not explain here the details of patent law or the intricacies of how to create and run a business based on your invention. Before devoting your time, energy, and economic resources to an invention, it is appropriate to figure out the relationship between what you might put into the invention and what you expect to get out of it. In this sense, launching an invention is the same as starting a business—in both situations you should carefully calculate your profit potential before you get in too deeply. It is this activity that we refer to when we later speak of creating a business plan for your invention.

Nolo also publishes *Patent It Yourself*, an excellent source of detailed information on obtaining and using a patent. For a full understanding of the legal principles associated with the information you will be entering in *The Inventor's Notebook*, we recommend that you obtain a copy of this comprehensive and clearly written resource. It is widely available in libraries and bookstores and can also be obtained by ordering directly from Nolo. See the Nolo catalog and ordering information at the back of this book.

In *Patent It Yourself*, author David Pressman has formulated 16 statements or instructions (termed Inventor's Commandments) that focus the reader's attention on the crucial steps necessary to the successful development of his or her invention. Throughout *The Inventor's Notebook* we provide cross-references to the relevant portions of *Patent It Yourself* and feature some of its "Inventor's Commandments" where appropriate.

In addition to *Patent It Yourself*, Nolo offers the following related materials:

- *Patent Searching Made Easy* by David Hitchock
- *Make Patent Drawings Yourself* by Patent Agent Jack Lo and Attorney David Pressman
- *License Your Invention* by Attorney Richard Stim
- *Patent, Copyright & Trademark* by Attorney Stephen Elias
- *Nolo's Patents for Beginners* by Attorneys David Pressman and Richard Stim
- *Market Your Invention*, an eFormKit by Attorney Richard Stim
- *PatentPro Plus*, a software program on CD-ROM.

These resources are available at the Nolo website (www.nolo.com). We also suggest you consult *How to Write a Business Plan* by Michael McKeever (Nolo).

C. How The Inventor's Notebook Is Organized

The Inventor's Notebook is designed to focus your attention on all major activities associated with successful inventing, and on the documentation that is appropriate and necessary to each. As our organizing tool we use the Inventor's Decision Chart from *Patent It Yourself* (see facing page).

As you can see, the chart presents a concise overview of the basic steps of the inventive process.

In the real world, of course, an invention can go from idea to marketplace in a great variety of ways. However, the paths outlined in the Inventor's Decision Chart serve as logical guidelines to the way in which a large percentage of

Inventor's Decision Chart

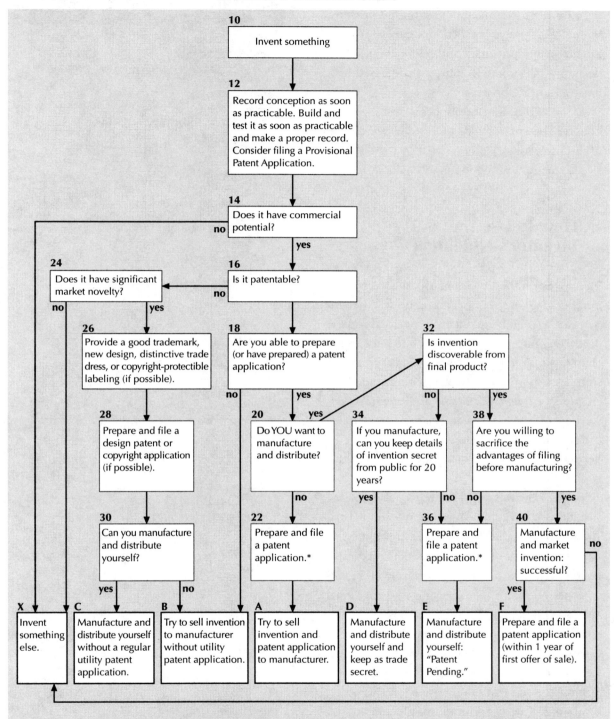

* If you filed a Provisional Patent Application, you must file a regular patent application and any desired foreign convention applications within one year—see *Patent It Yourself*, Chapter 3. (File non-Convention applications before invention is made public or any patent issues on it.)

inventing efforts will tend to develop, primarily because the fundamental questions addressed by the chart—legal protection, financial feasibility, marketing potential, and perfecting the final design of the product—must be addressed in most instances.

At the end of this introduction, we offer a brief description of the different paths represented in the Inventor's Decision Chart. A more extensive discussion can be found in *Patent It Yourself*.

D. How to Use The Inventor's Notebook

The boxes on the Inventor's Decision Chart are numbered 10, 12, 14, and so on up to 40, then A-F and X. Each box contains a brief description of its step and provides a cross-reference to the chapters in *Patent It Yourself* which discuss the step. Each step is discussed in one or more chapters of *Patent It Yourself* and one or more sections of *The Inventor's Notebook*. The Table of Cross-References below shows the links between boxes on the chart and the text in the two books.

To see how this cross-reference table works, assume you have conceived an invention (Box 10) and now are at Box 12 of the inventive process (record conception as soon as practicable, build and test it as soon as practicable and make a proper record, or consider filing a Provisional Patent Application). The Table of Cross-References tells you that you should read Chapter 1, Section B, Record Your Conception; Chapter 1, Section C, Record the Building and Testing of Your Invention or Section D, File a Provisional Patent Application); Chapter 1, Section E, Other Possible Applications of Your Invention; Chapter 2, Section H, Record of

Table of Cross-References		
Inventor's Decision Chart	*Inventor's Notebook* (Chapter & Section)	*Patent It Yourself* (Chapter)
#10	1B, 1E, 2H	1, 2
#12	1B, 1C, 1D, 1E, 2H, 3A, 4A	1, 3
#14	1B, 1C, 2B, 2E, 3C, 3E	4
#16	2A, 2B	5, 6
#18	2D, 2E, 2H, 2I, 4A	1, 8
#20	3E, 3F, 4A, 4C	11
#22	2A, 2B, 2D, 2E, 2H, 2I	6, 8, 9, 10, 12, 13, 14, 15
#24	2A, 2B, 3A, 3B, 3C	4
#26	1F, 1G, 2F	1
#28	1G, 2E, 2F	10
#30	3E, 3F, 4A, 4C	11
#32	2H, 2I	1
#34	2H, 2I	1
#36	2D, 2E, 2H, 2I	6, 8, 9, 10, 12, 13, 14, 15
#38	2H, 2I, 3E, 4A	7
#40	—	7
A	2H, 2I, 3F, 4B	11, 15, 16
B	2A, 2B, 2H, 2I, 3F, 4B	1, 11
C	—	1, 11
D	2H	1, 11
E	2H	1, 11, 15
F	2C	6, 8, 9, 10, 12, 13, 14, 15
X	Begin a new *Inventor's Notebook*	2

Contacts; Chapter 3, Section A, Evaluation of Positive and Negative Factors of Invention; and Chapter 4, Section A, Determination of Funds Needed.

Now let's take a brief look at what each of the sections listed in the chart for this example calls for.

1. Record Your Conception (Chapter 1, Section B)

Chapter 1, Section B, provides specific guidelines as to how to record your conception.

2. Record the Building and Testing of Your Invention (Chapter 1, Section C)

This section explains the importance of recording your efforts to build and test your invention. The better this documentation, the easier it will be for you to apply for a patent and the better your legal position will be if:

- you ever get into an inventorship dispute (one person claims that another person stole the invention from the first person);
- an interference is declared (a contest initiated in the Patent and Trademark Office when two patent applications from different inventors claim the same invention); or
- you need to swear behind a cited reference (i.e., show that you conceived or built and tested the invention before the date of a reference that would otherwise be "prior art" to your invention).

When determining whether your invention is sufficiently innovative under the Patent Act (i.e.,

that it's novel and nonobvious), the Patent and Trademark Office (PTO) and your adversaries in any court case will examine all known references that bear on your claims. It is very important to show that your earliest effective date of invention (patent application filing date, building and testing date, or date when you first began to diligently work towards building and testing) occurred prior to all such references; otherwise, your claims can be rejected on them.

3. File a Provisional Patent Application (Chapter 1, Section D)(optional)

An inventor can file a Provisional Patent Application (PPA) as an alternative to building and testing the invention. The PPA will serve as an alternative only if the inventor files a regular patent application within one year that claims the same invention disclosed in the PPA. If the regular patent application is filed within one year, the regular application may claim the PPA's filing date.

4. Other Possible Applications (Chapter 1, Section E)

This section asks you to focus on possible applications of your work which differ from those you have imagined.

5. Record of Contacts (Chapter 2, Section H)

This section permits you to keep track of all the people who know of your invention and who have signed confidentiality agreements. This information will be essential if a dispute arises later over inventorship or if you wish to take action against others under the trade secret laws for violation of a confidentiality agreement. (Many inventors maintain their invention as a trade secret until such time as the patent application is published (see sidebar, Publication of Patent Applications) or, if the application is not published, a patent issues or the invention is manufactured and placed on the market. This allows the inventor to take action against anyone who discloses the details of the invention to others in violation of a confidentiality agreement.)

6. Evaluation of Positive and Negative Factors of Invention (Chapter 3, Section A)

This section guides you in evaluating the positive and negative factors of your invention

so that you can make refinements while building and testing it.

7. Determination of Funds Needed (Chapter 4, Section A)

Finally, this section lets you document any special financial needs for the building and testing phase.

To sum up this example, Box 12 of the Table of Cross-References directs you to the sections of this book you should use for recording your conception and either documenting the building and testing of your invention or filing a Provisional Patent Application. As you proceed through the chart, other boxes will similarly direct you to other appropriate sections of this book. Careful documentation of your invention process will save time in the long run. Your organized approach will make it easy to retrieve essential information when you need it, and

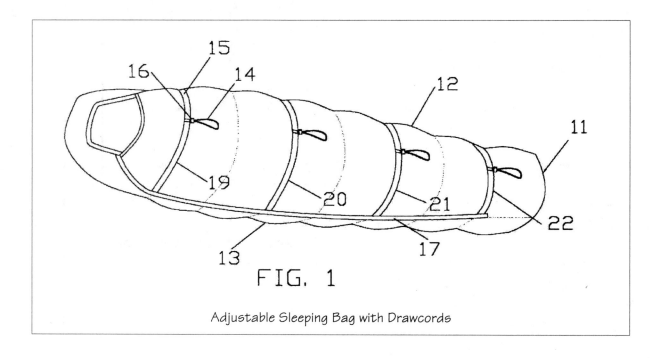

FIG. 1

Adjustable Sleeping Bag with Drawcords

you will be able to prove your inventorship if called on to do so.

DIRECT ACCESS NOTE
You can directly access *The Inventor's Notebook* without going through the Inventor's Decision Chart if you already understand what documentation is needed. Simply turn to the relevant form and enter the appropriate information. For guidance on the type of documentation needed to protect your invention, read the relevant portions of *Patent It Yourself* (or other resources recommended by us) which are referenced at the beginning of each section of Chapter 1.

WARNING
You are responsible for understanding the legal requirements for documentation and what steps have to be taken to obtain a patent and protect your invention from theft or unauthorized use. While we preface each section with a very brief overview of what should be entered there, and why it should be entered, this is not a substitute for reading the meticulous discussion of these issues provided by *Patent It Yourself*.

E. Explanation of Inventor's Decision Chart

As we mentioned, different inventions take different paths through the Inventor's Decision Chart. Here we outline the various paths. If you are not using the Inventor's Decision Chart as an organizational guide to this book, you may skip this discussion.

1. Drop It If You Don't See Commercial Potential (Chart Route 10-12-14-X)

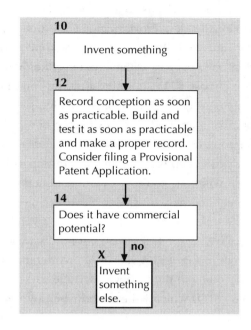

Publication of Patent Applications

If you are relying on trade secrecy or patent protection, your invention decision may be influenced by a change in the patent laws. Effective December 2000, every pending patent application will be published for the public to view 18 months after its earliest effective filing date (or earlier if requested by the applicant), unless, at the time of filing, the applicant files a Non-Publication Request. This publication will terminate any trade secrecy rights in the claimed invention. An applicant whose application is published and later issues as a patent may obtain royalties from an infringer from the date of publication if the infringer had actual notice of the published application.

If you've invented something and recorded it properly, you should then proceed to build and test your invention as soon as practicable and/or optionally file a Provisional Patent Application (PPA) and then file a regular patent application within one year that claims the PPA filing date. If you choose to build and test the invention and this presents appreciable difficulty, you should wait until after you evaluate your invention's commercial potential or patentability. But always keep the building and testing as a goal; it will help you to evaluate commercial potential and may be vital in the event an "interference" occurs (unless you file a valid PPA; see Chapter 1, Section D, for a discussion on what makes a PPA valid). An interference is a proceeding in the Patent and Trademark Office (PTO) which is instituted when two or more applications by separate inventors claim the same invention. It usually occurs when a patent examiner in the PTO discovers two pending applications which claim the same invention. It can also occur when the PTO publishes a newly granted patent in the *Official Gazette* and another inventor claims to have invented it first. Since interferences are long and expensive proceedings, the more convincing a party's documentation is, the better the chance to win and shorten an interference. You'll find a working model extremely valuable when you show the invention to a manufacturer.

Your next step is to investigate your invention's commercial potential. Assuming you decide that your invention has no commercial potential and you answer the question "no," follow an arrow to Box X, which says "Invent something else." In this instance, this sort of structured analysis may seem simplistic. It's not. In our direct experience we have seen hundreds of inventors waste thousands of hours because they would not confront the issue of "commercial potential" or lack thereof at an early stage of the invention process.

2. Try to Sell Invention to Manufacturer Without "Regular" Patent Application (Chart Route 12-14-16-18-B)

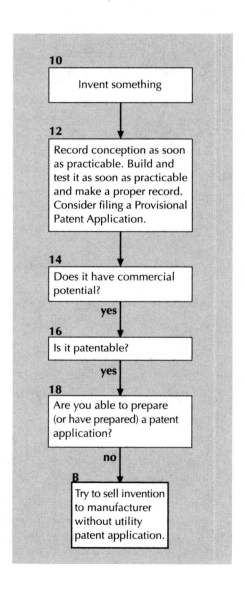

This route is especially useful if you've filed a PPA on the invention, but can also be used if you've built and tested the invention and properly recorded your building and testing activities. After filing a PPA and/or building and testing and recording your efforts, see if the invention has commercial potential and if it's patentable. If so, whether or not you're able to prepare—or have prepared—a regular patent application, try to sell your invention to a manufacturer in the hope that the manufacturer will have the application prepared for you, either on the basis of your PPA or without the PPA. If you take this route, you should be sure either that your PPA is properly prepared or that you've properly documented conception, building, and testing. We recommend this route only if you can't prepare or can't afford to have prepared a regular patent application because:

- if you've built and tested the invention without properly recording your activities, you run the risk of an unscrupulous manufacturer stealing your invention by filing a patent application on your invention before you do so, and
- if you've filed a PPA, you'll have all of the disadvantages of the PPA (see Chapter 1, Section D, for more discussion of the advantages and disadvantages of filing a PPA).

3. File a Patent Application and Sell or License It to a Manufacturer (Chart Route 14-16-18-20-22-A)

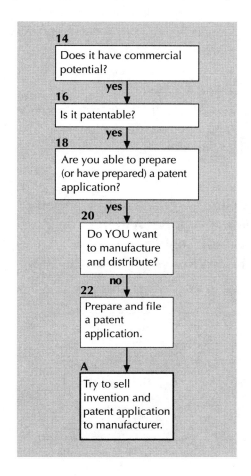

Filing a patent application and selling rights to the invention to someone else is the usual way most inventors profit from their work. This is because inventors seldom have the capability (and often don't have the desire) to establish their own manufacturing and distribution facilities. If you are in this situation, the chart works like this:

- Box 14—your invention has good commercial potential
- Box 16—your decision on patentability is favorable

- Box 18—you're able to prepare a regular patent application (or have one prepared for you)
- Box 20—you don't wish to manufacture and distribute your product or process yourself
- Box 22—you prepare a regular patent application, and
- Box A—you try to sell your invention (and accompanying patent application) to a manufacturer.

4. Sell or License Your Invention to a Manufacturer Without Filing a Patent Application (Chart Route 16-24-26-28-30-B)

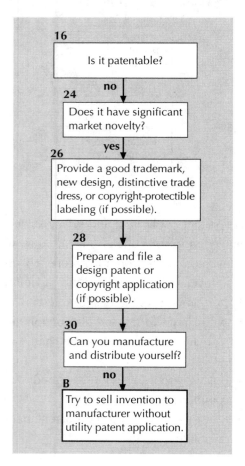

If your invention isn't patentable, don't give up. There's still hope that you can profit from your work. If your invention nevertheless possesses "significant market novelty," it may in fact be quite profitable if introduced to the market. Put differently, if your patentability search produces close "prior art" (but not a dead ringer), this may indicate that no one has tried to market your specific idea before.

Prior art is the sum of all developments prior to your conception which are used to determine whether your efforts were really inventive and "unobvious." Examples of prior art (relevant to your invention) are (1) prior patents showing your invention or any part or feature of it, (2) prior and related technological developments which are known to the public, (3) previous descriptions of your invention (or any part or feature of it) in periodicals or textbooks, and (4) previous indications of any kind that others considered some or all of your invention's elements. For example, the prior art which precludes you from getting a patent may have only been used to make computer screens, while your invention is designed for lampshades.

Assuming that your invention does have significant market novelty but does not qualify for protection under a utility patent, you may consider protecting it under trademark law; with a design patent; through distinctive "trade dress," such as a uniform color (as Kodak does with its yellow film packages); or with a symbol (such as the McDonald's golden arch).

5. Make and Sell Your Invention Yourself Without a Utility Patent Application (Chart Route 16-30-C)

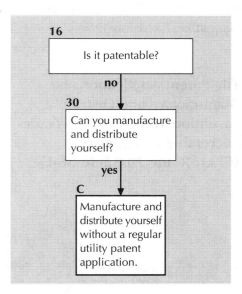

Here we assume again that you have an unpatentable invention which is unique and serves a useful purpose (there isn't anything on the market just like it and people will buy it). If you can make and distribute it yourself, it may be better to do so than to try to sell it to a manufacturer outright. Even if you have a good trademark, a design patent application, distinctive trade dress, and/or a unique label, you cannot offer a manufacturer a truly privileged market position on your invention unless it's covered by a utility patent application that looks like it will lead to a patent being granted. This means it will probably be hard to sell your invention to a third party, and if you do, the amount you receive for it will be modest. However, if you decide to manufacture the invention yourself, and you reach the market first, you'll have a significant marketing advantage despite the lack of a utility patent.

6. Manufacture and Distribute Your Invention Yourself, Keeping It As a Trade Secret (Chart Route 20-32-34-D)

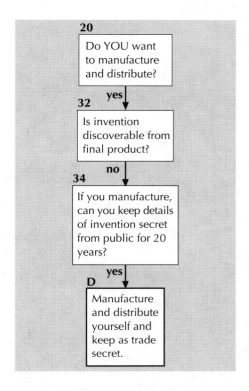

Even though your invention may be commercially valuable and patentable, it isn't always in your best interest to patent it. Instead you may profit more by keeping the invention secret and using it in your business to obtain a competitive advantage. For instance, suppose you invent a formula that truly makes hair grow. Instead of seeking a patent, which would require public disclosure of your formula and invite others to figure out why your formula works and perhaps invent alternatives, you might be better off keeping your formula locked in your safe and only disclose it to a few trusted associates who would be sworn to secrecy. For more on trade secret protection for inventions, see Chapter 1 of *Patent It Yourself.*

7. File Patent Application and Manufacture and Distribute Your Invention Yourself (Trade-Secretable Invention) (Chart Route 20-32-34-36-E)

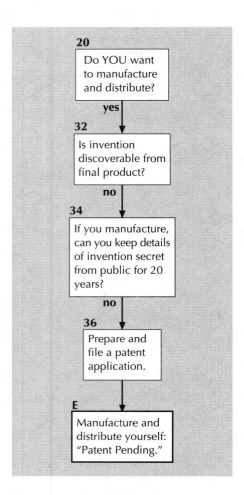

against the trade secret protection route, preferring instead to patent your invention. Either way, you should prepare and file a patent application and then manufacture and distribute the invention yourself with the notice "patent pending" affixed to the invention.

8. File Patent Application and Manufacture and Distribute Invention Yourself (Non–Trade-Secretable Invention) (Chart Route 20-32-38-36-E)

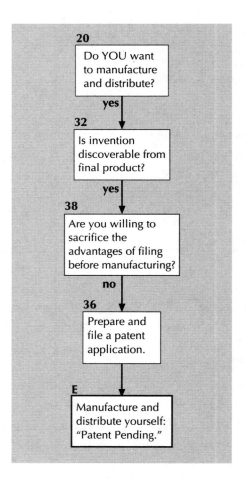

Suppose the essence of your invention is not easily discoverable from your final product so that you could keep it secret for a while, but probably not for the life of a patent. Or, suppose, after evaluating the advantages and disadvantages of maintaining your invention as a trade secret (Section 6 above), you decide

This is the route followed by most inventors who wish to manufacture their own invention. Assume that the essence of your invention, like most, is discoverable from the final product. In this case you won't be able to protect it as a trade secret. Also assume that you don't want to sacrifice the advantages of filing before manufacturing (number 9 below). You should prepare and file a patent application and then manufacture and distribute the invention yourself with a patent-pending notice.

9. Test-Market Before Filing (Chart Route 20-32-38-40-F)

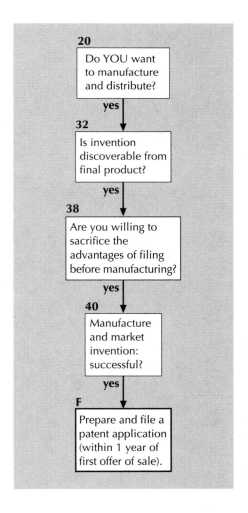

Although you might like to manufacture and test-market your invention before filing a patent application on it, we generally don't recommend this for patentable inventions. This is because, under the "one-year rule," you have less than one year to do the test-marketing before your patent application must be filed. This very important rule is based upon a statute which states that, with certain exceptions, you must file your patent application within one year after the invention was exposed to the public. Since one year is a relatively short time, you may get discouraged unjustifiably if you try to market your invention and you aren't successful. Also, you'll lose your foreign rights, since most foreign countries or jurisdictions, including the European Patent Office, have an "absolute novelty" requirement (which means no patent will be issued if the invention was made public anywhere before its first filing date). Lastly, there is a possibility of theft, since anyone who sees it can copy it (assuming it's not trade secretable) and file a (fraudulent) patent application on it. There are also other significant disadvantages to test-marketing an invention.

Nevertheless, you may still choose to manufacture and market your invention before filing your patent application. If you discover, within about nine months of the date you first introduce your product, that it is a successful invention and likely to have good commercial success, begin immediately to prepare your patent application, so that you'll be able to get it on file within one year from the date you first offered your invention for sale or used it to make a commercial product.

If your manufacturing and market tests are not successful, you should consider dropping the invention and inventing something else, even though you still have the right to get a patent on your invention. On the other hand, as we stated above, a nine-month testing period may not have been adequate. In other words, be realistic but don't get discouraged unnecessarily from filing a patent application. ■

1

Using the Notebook

A well-maintained notebook will be of crucial importance should your inventorship or your eligibility for a patent ever be called into question by the Patent and Trademark Office, other inventors, or companies which you have sued for infringement.

A. How to Make Entries

When using Appendix I: Notebook, it is important to remember that the more secure your notebook appears to be from the possibility of after-the-fact modifications by you, the better evidence it is. The first step in achieving this credibility is to use a bound notebook like this one. Your textual entries, sketches, and diagrams should be clearly written in ink to preclude erasure and the making of later entries. No large blank spaces should be left on a page. If you do need to leave space between separate entries, or at the bottom of a page, draw a large cross over the blank space to preclude the possibility of any subsequent entries. If you make a mistake in an entry, don't attempt to erase it; merely line it out neatly and make a dated note of why it was incorrect. Your entries should be worded carefully and accurately to be complete and clear in themselves so that a disinterested person could verify that you had the ideas or did the work stated on the dates in question.

Where we indicate, your entries in Appendix I should be signed, dated, and witnessed. This should be done frequently. You should date each entry the same day you (and any co-inventors) make the entries and sign your name(s). If it is impossible to have a witness sign the same day you do, add a brief candid comment to this effect when the witness does sign. Similarly, if you made and/or built the invention some time ago, but haven't made any records until now, again state the full and truthful facts and date the entry as of the date you write and sign it. Remember, though, that entries made contemporaneously with your work or ideas will carry much more weight than after-the-fact entries, should you ever have to prove prior inventorship.

If possible, items that by their nature can't be entered directly in the Notebook by hand should be made on separate sheets. These, too, should be signed, dated, and witnessed and then pasted or affixed in the Notebook in proper chronological order. The inserted sheet should be referred to by entries made directly in the Notebook, thus tying them in to the other material. Photos or other entries which cannot be signed or written should be pasted in the Notebook and referenced by legends (descriptive words, such as "photo taken of machine in operation") made directly in the Notebook, preferably with lead lines which extend from the Notebook page over onto the photo, so as to preclude a charge of substituting subsequently made photos. The page the photo is pasted on should be signed, dated, and witnessed in the usual manner.

If an item covers an entire page, it can be referred to on an adjacent page. It's important to affix the items to the Notebook page with a permanent adhesive, such as white glue or non-yellowing transparent tape.

If you have to draw a sketch in pencil and want to make a permanent record of it (to put in your Notebook) without redrawing the sketch in ink, simply make a photocopy of the penciled sketch: Voilà—a permanent copy!

Finally, if there are more than two inventors, make a new space for each additional inventor to sign.

Choose witnesses who are as impartial and competent as possible, which means that ideally they should not be close relatives or people who have been working so closely with you as to be possible co-inventors. Witnesses should also be people who are likely to be available to testify later, should a dispute over your inventorship arise.

B. Record Your Conception

 Recommended Reading
Patent It Yourself, Chapter 3

There are many reasons to accurately record the date and surrounding circumstances of your original conception of your invention. The most important of these is to have proof that you are the true inventor in case another inventor claims prior inventorship. Recording your conception in the manner we suggest here is like giving your invention a pedigree. With proper records, your invention will be recognized as yours; without this documentary evidence, your invention's special identity and origins are subject to challenge.

There are a number of elements involved in recording the conception of your invention. These are:

- your invention's title
- the circumstances of its conception
- its purpose or the problem solved
- a brief functional and structural description of the invention as you have conceived it
- an informal sketch
- all possible applications of your invention (ramifications)
- your invention's novel features, insofar as you know them now

- a brief description of the closest known prior art, and
- the advantages of the invention over previous developments and/or knowledge in the relevant field.

We can't overemphasize the importance of accurately documenting the conception of your invention, which is summed up in this Inventor's Commandment from *Patent It Yourself.*

Inventor's Commandment

After conceiving of your invention, you should not proceed to develop, build, or test it, or reveal it to outsiders until you first:

1. make a clear description of your conception
2. sign and date the same, and
3. have this document signed and dated by two people you trust to the effect that they have "witnessed and understood" your creation. (As an alternative to documenting conception in this matter, you can use the PTO's Document Disclosure Program, but be aware of the disadvantages and limitations of the DDP. See sidebar, Document Conception Using the Disclosure Document Program (DDP), below)

Following this commandment will help you:

- prove prior conception in case of an interference or theft of your idea
- establish your inventorship in case someone else claims inventorship, and
- antedate any prior art which may be cited by the Patent and Trademark Office (PTO) that may cast doubt on the originality of your invention. (A prior art reference is

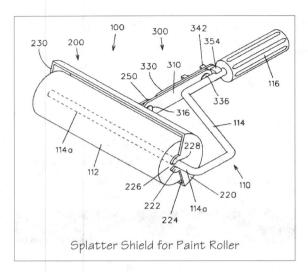

Splatter Shield for Paint Roller

any previous patent, article, or other document or actual public knowledge or use which is relevant to the PTO's decision on whether your invention deserves a patent.)

 Record of Conception pages are located in Appendix I: Notebook.

If you use no other part of this book, we urge you to provide the documentation we suggest here. When filling out this form, remember our instructions for making entries set out in the introduction to this chapter.

You should only use this form when you have arrived at a relatively firm idea of what your invention consists of. Then, if you change your approach or think of additional complications after you have recorded your conception but prior to your building and testing activity, put these new ideas on the blank pages provided for this specific purpose at the end of the Record of Conception pages.

A sample record of the conception of an invention is provided on the following pages.

Document Conception Using the Disclosure Document Program (DDP)

As an alternative to documenting conception by notebook entries, the Patent and Trademark Office (PTO) has a program, the Document Disclosure Program (DDP), under which it accepts Invention Disclosures. The purpose of this service, for which the PTO charges a small fee (see Appendix IV, Fee Schedule), is to provide credible evidence of the conception date and inventorship for inventors who, for some reason, cannot or don't wish to rely on witnesses.

This program is advantageous for an inventor who does not use a lab notebook or wish to rely on witnesses. The disadvantage is that if an inventor files a disclosure document and does nothing else, the PTO will destroy it after two years. Therefore, an inventor who plans to file a patent application based on the disclosure must do so within two years of filing. For this reason, some patent experts prefer to document conception using a notebook instead of the DDP.

To file a DDP, the inventor sends the signed document, a cover letter, a check for the fee (see Appendix IV, Fee Schedule), and a stamped return receipt postcard. The procedures and form for filing a disclosure document is provided in Chapter 3 of *Patent It Yourself*.

Even if you use the DDP to record your conception, you should still use a notebook or separate sheets with proper witnessing to record all the pertinent facts if you build and test your invention. Finally, filing a disclosure document with the PTO doesn't allow you to refer to the invention as "Patent Pending" or "Patent Applied For." (It's actually a criminal offense, punishable by a $500 fine, to refer to an invention as "Patent Pending" where no provisional or regular patent application has been filed.)

Record of Conception of Invention

Title of invention:

"Orange Peeling Knife" or "knife that can score oranges through skin without cutting pulp."

Circumstances of conception:

On March 2 or 3 of this year, when visiting my sister Shirley Goldberger in Lancaster, PA, I decided to eat orange just before we all went shopping. When I tried to score through the orange's skin to peel it, I cut too deeply, and the juice dripped onto my lap. It stained my new pants and embarrassed me in front of Shirley, my wife and my mother. I had to change my pants, delaying everyone in the process.

   After we eventually got in the car, I remarked that there must be a better way to score and peel oranges. The problem preoccupied me so much that I didn't go shopping; instead, I came up with a solution while waiting in my car for my family. I remember telling them, on the way back, "Why not make a knife with an adjustable blade stop so that the depth of the cut could be controlled? That way you wouldn't cut into the orange's pulp, it would be easier to peel and it wouldn't drip."

   I didn't make any record of the invention at that time since I didn't know I should until I read this book yesterday.

Purpose or problem solved:

To peel oranges (or grapefruits or pomelos), it is desirable to score them first, preferably with two encircling cuts that cross at the blossom and stem ends so that the skin can be neatly peeled off in quarters. However, this is difficult with an ordinary knife because one inevitably cuts past the skin into the pulp, making the orange drip and the peel difficult to remove without removing some of the pulp with it. The problem is compounded because the thickness of orange peels varies among varieties. A tool that could neatly score oranges with peels of various thicknesses without cutting into the pulp would solve the problem.

Invented by: _Edward R. Furman_   Date: _July 23, 200—_
Invented by: _____   Date: _____
The above confidential information is witnessed and understood by:
   Ruben Santiago   Date: _July 23, 200—_
                                                    Date: _____

Record of Conception of Invention

Description and operation:

My knife will have a handle and blade similar to those on a conventional paring knife. Attached to each side of the blade, however, will be a strip of plastic or wood that will serve as a stop or fence to control the depth of cuts that can be made with the knife. These fences will be moveable, allowing the depth of the cut to be varied by adjustments made to a thumbscrew that will be attached to the two fences. For thin-skinned oranges, the fences will be adjusted to permit a shallow cut, and for thick-skinned oranges, the fences will be adjusted to allow a deeper cut. In either case, the knife will be easily used to score through the skin completely around the orange without cutting deeper than the distance from the edge of the blade to the fences, and thus without cutting its pulp.

Invented by: _Edward R. Furman_   Date: _July 23, 200—_

Invented by: _____   Date: _____

The above confidential information is witnessed and understood by:

Ruben Santiago   Date: _July 23, 200—_

_____   Date: _____

Record of Conception of Invention

Drawing:

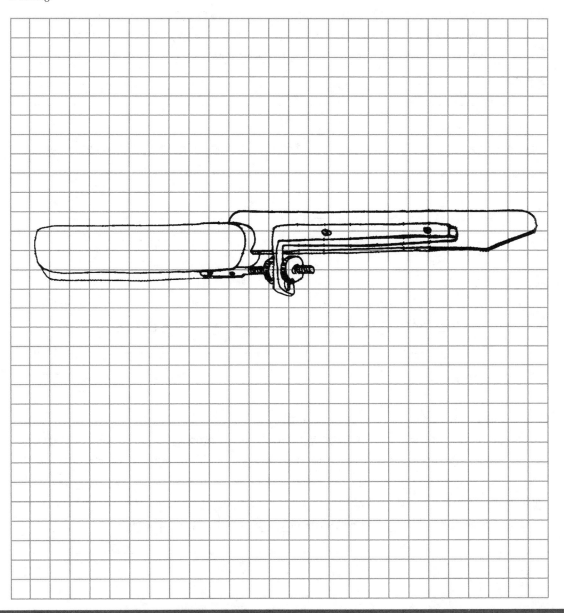

Invented by: _Edward R. Furman_   Date: _July 23, 200—_

Invented by: _____   Date: _____

The above confidential information is witnessed and understood by:

Ruben Santiago   Date: _July 23, 200—_

_____   Date: _____

Record of Conception of Invention

Ramifications:

Instead of adjustable stop strips on both sides of the blade, a fixed stop strip, on one or both sides, can be used. This fixed stop strip can be mounted parallel to the edge, or it can even be included on the edge so that the depth of cut can be controlled by changing the longitudinal part of the blade that contacts the orange.

Novel features:

I have never seen or heard of any knife with a depth-of-cut controlling stop strip, much less an adjustable one.

Closest known prior art:

I have seen orange peelers comprising a curved knife and a curved metal rod that is inserted under the peel to move it around and free the peel from the pulp; and, of course, conventional paring knives.

Advantages of my invention:

My knife is the only one that can cut through an orange's peel to any desired depth. It makes peeling an orange neater, safer, and faster. All one has to do is score around the skin with two encircling cuts and then peel off the four quarter peels, leaving a peeled orange that is ready to segment and eat. The messy and difficult-to-use prior-art methods, which involve cutting the orange in quarters and peeling off the pulp, are tools that require skill to use and are not nearly as fast, neat and easy to use as mine.

Invented by: _Edward R. Furman_   Date: _July 23, 200—_

Invented by: _____ Date: _____

The above confidential information is witnessed and understood by:

Ruben Santiago   Date: _July 23, 200—_

_____ Date: _____

C. Record the Building and Testing of Your Invention

 Recommended Reading
Patent It Yourself, Chapter 3

Record of Building and Testing of Invention pages are located in Appendix I: Notebook.

Inventor's Commandment

1. Try to build and test your invention (if at all possible) as soon as you can.
2. Keep full and true written, signed, and dated records of all the efforts, correspondence, and receipts concerning your invention, especially if you build and test it.
3. Have two others sign and date that they have "witnessed and understood" your building and testing.

When documenting the building and testing of your invention, you should record as much factual data about the process as possible. Provide conclusions only if they are supported by factual data. Items that by their nature can't be entered directly in the Notebook by hand—such as formal sketches or photos—should be signed, dated, and witnessed and then pasted or affixed in the Notebook in proper chronological order. You should also save all of your "other paperwork" involved with the conception, building, and testing of your invention, such as loose notes, bedside notes, receipts, letters, memos, etc. These items can be very convincing as supporting evidence to a judge if you ever need to prove any of the pertinent dates related to your invention. Because of the potential importance of this documentation, do yourself a favor and provide a place to save these papers. We suggest that you paste a 6" x 9" manila envelope inside the back cover of this book or use an expansion pocket file if the papers become too voluminous.

If you build and test your invention immediately after you conceive of it, fill out the Record of Conception and add a brief note indicating that you also built and tested it at the same time. Make a reference to and then complete the Record of Building and Testing of Invention, which is also in Appendix I: Notebook.

If you can't build and test your invention yourself, many model makers, engineers, technicians, teachers, etc., are available who will be delighted to do the job for you for a fee, or for a percentage of the action. If you do use a model maker (consultant), you should take precautions to protect the confidentiality and proprietary status of your invention. There's no substitute for checking out your consultant carefully by asking for references (assuming you don't already know the consultant by reputation or referral).

In addition, have your consultant sign a copy of the Consultant's Work Agreement included in Appendix V: Tear-Out Forms. See Chapter 4F of *Patent It Yourself* for instructions on completing this form.

When providing this documentation, remember to follow the instructions given at the beginning of this chapter.

D. File a Provisional Patent Application

Suppose you don't have the facilities, skill, or time to build and test your invention and you can't file a patent application right away. In 1994 the government enacted the GATT (General Agreement on Tariffs and Trade) implementation law, which, for the first time in the U.S., enables an inventor to file a Provisional Patent Application (PPA) as a legal alternative to building and testing the invention. Let's explore the PPA and its advantages and disadvantages.

What it is

A PPA is a short version of a patent application which an applicant can use to establish an early filing date for a later-filed Regular Patent Application (RPA). A PPA consists of the following:

- a detailed description of the invention telling how to make and use it
- drawing(s), if necessary to understand how to make and use the invention
- a cover sheet, and
- a fee.

What it is not

For those readers already familiar with the regular patent application process (See Chapter 2, Section E), unlike an RPA, a PPA does not require:

- a Patent Application Declaration (PAD)
- an Information Disclosure Statement (IDS)
- claims
- an abstract and summary
- a description of the invention's background, or

- a statement of the invention's objects and advantages.

Your PPA cannot by itself result in a patent. If you don't file an RPA within a year of your PPA's filing date, your PPA will go abandoned and will be forever useless. Also, your PPA cannot provide a filing date for subject matter that is not disclosed in it.

What type of detailed description is necessary for a valid PPA?

Your PPA must disclose clearly and fully how to make and use the invention. That is, it must have the same level of detail that is required in the part of the Specification section of a regular patent application where you describe the invention's main embodiment and operation.

When to file a PPA

We recommend that you file a PPA only if:

- you want to establish an early filing date because you feel your invention is potentially valuable and might be independently developed by others or stolen from you
- you can't or don't want to build and test your invention now, and
- you can't or don't want to file an RPA on it now.

Additional reasons to file a PPA are:

- You can file a PPA, and then file an RPA within one year, which has the practical effect of delaying examination of the RPA and extending—up to one year—your patent's expiration date.
- You can file an RPA, convert it to a PPA one year later, and then file a second RPA based upon the PPA to extend your patent's expiration date for two years.

Reasons you may not wish to file a PPA are:

- You may tend to forego building and testing and lose the concomitant advantages, such as determining whether the invention is operable, practical, and useful, and having a working prototype to demonstrate to prospective manufacturers.
- The filing fee is not insignificant (as of September, 2000, $75 for small entities, $150 for large entities).
- Your PPA must contain a full a description of the actual nuts and bolts of the invention, and how it will operate. Just as with an RPA, absent this description, the PPA will have no legal effect.
- You cannot wait one year after filing the RPA to foreign file. Instead you must make your foreign filing decision, as well as your regular U.S. filing decision, within one year after your PPA is filed.

See Chapter 2, Section D, for the steps necessary to prepare a PPA.

E. Other Possible Applications of Your Invention

Recommended Reading
Patent it Yourself, Chapter 2

As you proceed to build and test your invention, you will probably have flashes of insight as to other possible uses for it. This section of the Notebook is designed specifically for you to immediately record these "bolts from the blue" so that later on, when you draft your patent application or formulate marketing plans, you can easily refer to them.

F. Record Your Trademark Conception

Recommended Reading
Patent It Yourself, Chapter 1

The brand name or design symbol (or both) that you attach to or associate with your invention for marketing purposes is known as a trademark. Needless to say, if your product is successful in the marketplace, your trademark can become very valuable.

 The Trademark Conception and Protection form in Appendix I: Notebook is provided for recording a drawing or description of any trademark you create. We provide space for four trademark conceptions in case a trademark search reveals a conflict.

For each trademark you should provide the mark itself—a name, graphic design, or a name with a graphic design together with the generic descriptor "goods" or "service" with which the mark is to be used. For example, with Ivory soap, "IVORY" is the mark and "soap" is the goods or generic descriptor.

Although your proposed trademark will not be subject to protection under federal and state trademark laws until you either use it or apply to register it on the basis of intended use, it can be considered a trade secret until that time. Accordingly, we suggest these pages be signed, dated, and witnessed so you can prove that you came up with the name first in case of a trade secret dispute on this point. In Chapter 2, Section G, you can read how to record details as to the use and registration of your trademark in case of a later dispute over its ownership.

G. Record Your Distinctive Design Conception

 Recommended Reading
Patent it Yourself, Chapter 1

On the Distinctive Design Conception form in Appendix I: Notebook, you should enter any distinctive product designs you feel might qualify for either copyright or design patent protection.

By product design, we mean the shape of your invention, such as the shape of a computer case, the shape of a bottle, the design of jewelry, etc. We provide four pages for you to do this. You should record the conception and the building and testing of your design, just as you did for a utility invention. If, however, your design is already shown in the Record of Conception of Invention or the Record of Building and Testing of Invention documentation of your utility invention, then of course that will suffice and you don't have to make separate documentation records for the design.

If your invention has a distinctive design that is basically unrelated to its function, you may be able to protect the design from use by others by a design patent or copyright.

Design patents last for 14 years and give you the right to prevent others from using your distinctive design for that period of time, even if they created the design independently of you. (How to get a design patent is discussed in Chapter 10 of *Patent It Yourself.*) Copyright protection is usable for designs of toys and nonutilitarian articles, such as jewelry, or even utilitarian articles where the artwork is separable from the article, such as fabric design. Copyright protection lasts for your life plus 70 years (or for 95–120 years if the design was created as a work made for hire) and gives you the right to exclude others from copying your work. Each form of protection has some advantages and disadvantages. The primary advantage of the design patent is that it offers a broader scope of protection. The copyright, on the other hand, is much easier to create and maintain, and offers protection for a longer period of time. Because of the greater value of its advantages, we recommend that you use copyright protection for all toys, nonutilitarian articles and objects. If the object is utilitarian and its aesthetic features can't be separated from the article, use design patent protection. We recommend that you not try to obtain both forms of protection for one design. Asserting two "monopolies" over one creation may be construed by the courts as overreaching and may therefore result in a loss of protection for your design. ■

2

Legal Protection

This chapter describes how to organize and record the information you will need to obtain the fullest possible legal protection for your invention. It explains the following nine worksheets:

- The Prior Art Search worksheet helps you keep track of the prior art which will ultimately determine whether your invention receives a patent (and which you must disclose to the PTO as part of your patent application). This section also alerts you to any public use or exposure of your invention which might trigger the rule requiring filing of a patent application within one year of such public use or exposure.

- The Patentability Checklist helps you assess the patentability of your invention.

- The Document Disclosure Checklist keeps track of the elements required for filing a disclosure under the PTO's Disclosure Document Program.

- The Provisional Patent Appliction Checklist helps you make sure your Provisional Patent Application is complete.

- The Patent Application Checklist helps you keep track of the many items and steps involved in preparing and filing a complete patent application.

- The Design Patent Application Checklist helps you organize your effort to obtain a design patent.

- The Trademark Use and Registration documents the results of any trademark search you have conducted regarding your proposed trademark for your invention, the first use (if any) of the trademark, and information about steps you have taken to protect the trademark (registration and renewal with the PTO and state agencies).

- The Record of Contacts keeps track of all contacts you make with outside individuals and companies about your invention, and whether you have obtained confidentiality agreements (we call them Proprietary Materials Agreements) as appropriate. This information will help you maintain your invention as a trade secret pending the issuance of a patent.

- The Legal Protection Summary is a checklist which lets you know whether you have done what you should to legally protect your invention and trademark.

A. Prior Art Search

Recommended Reading
Patent It Yourself, Chapter 6
Patent Searching Made Easy by David Hitchcock (Nolo)

Inventor's Commandment
You should make (or have made) a thorough patentability search of your invention before you file a patent application.

Complete the Prior Art Search form in Appendix II: Worksheets to determine whether your invention is patentable (Box 16).

As you probably know, whether your invention is patentable depends in large part upon previous developments in the same field (prior art).

Most specialized inventors have a good working grasp of the relevant prior art and are able to come up with something different, at least to some degree. (Of course many inventors invent first and then check to see whether it qualifies for a patent.) Awareness of prior art usually comes from:

- reviewing previously issued patents
- researching trade journal articles, and
- carefully checking wholesale and retail channels to see whether a similar product has been marketed.

It is important for you to conduct a preliminary search of relevant prior art to determine whether your invention is sufficiently innovative to qualify for a patent. Keep careful track of the prior art references you accumulate in the course of your preliminary search. This is because later, when you file your patent application, you will need to list all prior art known to you. Documenting all prior art you discover as you go along will make your actual patent application process a whole lot easier.

This section also asks you to document the date your invention is first exposed to or used in public in a way that might trigger the one-year rule.

1. Locating Relevant Patents Online

You can locate information about previously issued patents by using online patent databases, such as the one at the PTO website (www. uspto.gov) or by using the facilities at the Patent and Trademark Depository Libraries (PTDLs) located in major cities (a complete listing of PTDLs is provided at the USPTO website (www.uspto.gov)).

Online searching is ideal for locating a specific patent and performing preliminary research. Beware, however, most online patent data banks usually go back only to 1971 or 1976, and it is possible that a patent issued before these dates might demonstrate the obviousness or lack of novelty for a new invention. This is not a problem for most high-tech inventions, because the relevant prior art is post-1960s. Despite its limitations, online searching has some obvious advantages such as cost and ease of use.

Free databases:

- **The U.S. Patent & Trademark Office** (www.uspto.gov/patft/index.html)—an online full-text searchable database of patents and drawings that cover the period from January 1976 to the most recent weekly issue date (usually each Tuesday). In order to view the drawings, your computer must be able to view TIFF files. The PTO's site is linked to a source that provides a free downloadable reader program. For faster searching there is also a Bibliographic Database that contains only the text of each patent without drawings.
- **Delphion** (www.delphion.com/)—an online searchable database with abstract, title, and claims searching capability for patents issued from 1974 to the present. Delphion also provides fee-based searching at U.S. patent applications and foreign patents.

Fee-based databases:

- **Micropatent** (www.micropatent.com)—
  U.S. and Japanese patents are searchable
  from 1976 to the present, International
  PCT patents from 1983, European patents
  from 1988, and the *Official Gazette*
  (Patents).
- **Patent Miner** (www.patentminer.com)—
  U.S. patents searchable from 1970 to the
  present. Copies of any patent dating from
  1790 can be acquired.
- **LexPat** (www.lexis-nexis.com)—U.S.
  patents searchable from 1971 to the
  present. In addition, the *LEXPAT* library
  offers extensive prior-art searching
  capability of technical journals and
  magazines.
- **QPAT** (www.qpat.com/)—U.S. patents
  searchable from 1974 to the present.

Several of the "for fee" databases provide
foreign patent information.

2. Obtaining Copies of Patents

You can order a copy of a patent by:

- clicking on "Order Copy" at the "Manual
  Search" page at the PTO website
  (www.uspto.gov);
- downloading a text copy or image copy
  of the patent from the IBM or PTO search
  sites;
- ordering a copy from a private supply
  company such as Faxpat
  (www.faxpat.com) or Corporate Intelli-
  gence (www.1790.com);
- if using facilities at a PTDL, by filling out
  a PTO patent copy order coupon; or
- writing a letter listing the number of the
  patent to "Commissioner for Patents,

Washington, DC 20231" with a check for
the price per patent (see Appendix IV:
Fee Schedule) times the total number of
patents you've ordered.

Inventor's Commandment

One-Year Rule: You should treat the "one-
year rule" as holy. You must file your patent
application within one year of the date on
which you first publish; publicly use; sell; or
offer your invention, or any product which
embodies same, for sale. Moreover, if you
wish to preserve your foreign rights and
frustrate pirates of your creation, you should
actually file your patent application before
you publish or sell your creation.

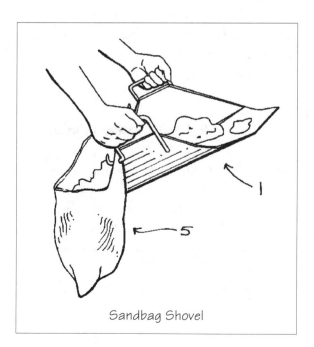

Sandbag Shovel

Determining an Invention's Classification

When performing patent searches, you will need to determine your invention's most relevant search classification (called class and subclass). Every type of invention is categorized in a class. For example, if you invented something that has to do with sewing, you would search in Class 112. If the invention had to do with sewing gloves, it would be in Class 112, Subclass 16. You can find the appropriate classifications in any of the following references, all of which are available at the USPTO website. These consist of:

- *Index to the U.S. Patent Classification*— lists all possible subject areas of invention alphabetically, from "abacus" to "zwieback," together with the appropriate class and subclass for each. The *Index* also lists the classes alphabetically.
- *Manual of Classification*—lists all classes numerically and subclasses under each class. After locating the class and subclass numbers, the *Manual of Classification* is used as an adjunct to the *Index*, to check the selected classes, and to find other, closely related ones.
- *Classification Definitions*—contains a definition for every class and subclass in the *Manual of Classification*. At the end of each subclass definition is a cross-reference of additional places to look that correspond to such subclass. Search classifications can also be obtained at a PTDL by using the CD-ROM CASSIS (Classification And Search Support Information System).

B. Patentability Checklist

Recommended Reading
Patent It Yourself, Chapter 5

Record the reasons why you believe your invention is patentable on the Patentability Checklist in Appendix II: Worksheets.

To be patentable, an invention must:
- fit within one of the statutory classes of patentable inventions
- be useful
- be novel, and
- be unobvious from the standpoint of one skilled in the relevant art.

By completing the checklist you will gain a preliminary understanding of whether your invention is patentable or whether any alternate form of legal protection should be sought. We provide three copies in Appendix II, as it is possible that you will come up with a number of versions of your invention in the course of prosecuting your patent application in the Patent and Trademark Office.

C. Document Disclosure Checklist

Recommended Reading
Patent It Yourself, Chapters 3, 8

Keep track of the components that make up an acceptable filing under the PTO's Disclosure Document Program on the Document Disclosure Checklist in Appendix II: Worksheets.

Keep in mind, the DDP won't do you any good unless a patent application is filed within two years. For more specific filing instructions, see Chapters 3 and 8 of *Patent It Yourself*. You need to:

1. Prepare a cover letter requesting that the attached disclosure be accepted under the Disclosure Document Program.
2. Prepare one copy of your Document Disclosure Checklist or Invention Disclosure form.
3. Write a check for the specified fee (see Appendix IV: Fee Schedule).
4. Prepare a stamped receipt postcard.
5. Send the items to Box DD, Commissioner for Patents, Washington, DC 20231. The disclosure sheets must be numbered and letter size (8½" x 11") or A4 size (210 mm x 297 mm). You should submit a photocopy of your original signed and witnessed disclosure and keep your original.

D. Provisional Patent Application Checklist

Recommended Reading
Patent It Yourself, Chapters 3, 8

The Provisional Patent Application Checklist in Appendix II: Worksheets keeps track of the basic components that make up a Provisional Patent Application (PPA). Check off each step of the process as it is completed.

Keep in mind, the PPA won't do you any good unless you adequately describe your invention in it and then file a regular patent application within one year. Also remember that your PPA filing date begins the one-year period you have to accomplish most foreign filings. See Chapter 3 of *Patent It Yourself* for specific filing instructions, and Chapter 8 of *Patent It Yourself* for instructions on how to adequately describe the structure and operation of your invention. You will need to:

1. Prepare drawings, if necessary
2. Describe your invention
3. Describe its operation
4. Prepare a cover letter
5. Write a check for the specified fee (see Appendix IV: Fee Schedule)
6. Prepare a stamped receipt postcard
7. Mail all papers to the PTO.

E. Patent Application Checklist

Recommended Reading
Patent It Yourself, Chapters 8, 13, 15

Inventor's Commandment

Your patent application must contain a description of your invention in such full, complete, clear, and exact terms, including details of your preferred embodiment at the time you file, so that anyone having ordinary skill in the field will be readily able to make and use it, and preferably so that even a lay judge will be able to understand it.

The Patent Application Checklist in Appendix II: Worksheets records the basic components which make up a patent application.

When you think you are ready to file your patent application, you will want to consult this list and see whether in fact you are ready to fulfill the requirements of each component.

You should check off (in the space provided) each step of the patent process as it is completed. This will help you know exactly where you stand in respect to your application as a whole.

After your patent application has been submitted, there will be additional transactions with the PTO. We also provide a checklist for the most common of these transactions.

F. Design Patent Application Checklist

 Recommended Reading
Patent It Yourself, Chapter 10

The Design Patent Application Checklist in Appendix II: Worksheets keeps track of the components which go into a design patent application.

If you have decided that a separate design patent is appropriate for your invention, you will want to consult this list and see whether you are ready to file. Again, check off each step as you complete it so that you can help keep track of where you are. You need to:

1. Prepare a Design Patent Application
2. Prepare drawings, if necessary
3. Prepare a Patent Application Declaration
4. Write a check for the filing fee (see Appendix IV: Fee Schedule)
5. Prepare a stamped receipt postcard
6. Prepare an Information Disclosure Statement and List of Prior Art Cited
7. Mail all papers to the PTO.

G. Trademark Use and Registration

The Trademark Use and Registration form in Appendix II: Worksheets documents the steps you should take to make sure this trademark is valid and cannot be used by competitors.

In Chapter 1, Section F, we ask you to describe the trademark (if any) under which you plan to market your invention. (For more information on all aspects of trademark law and comprehensive instructions on how to register a trademark, see *Trademark: Legal Care for Your Business and Product Name* by Attorney Stephen Elias (Nolo).)

The first step is to determine whether your proposed trademark is sufficiently distinguishable from existing trademarks to avoid later charges of trademark infringement. This effort (termed a trademark search) usually involves, at a minimum, an examination of:

- the list of trademarks registered (and pending registrations) with the Patent and Trademark Office
- the list of trademarks registered in your state
- existing product and service names (trademarks and service marks), and
- trade and product journals covering subjects related to your invention.

It is possible to conduct a preliminary online search to determine if your trademark is distinguishable from other federally registered trademarks. This can be accomplished using the PTO's free trademark databases (at the PTO's website www.uspto.gov) that provide free access to records of federally registered marks or marks that are pending (applications undergoing examination at the PTO). The PTO database does not include trademark applications filed during the last two to four months, nor does it contain any information on state, foreign, or common law trademarks or inactive applications and registrations (i.e., abandoned applications or canceled or expired registrations).

Privately owned fee-based online trademark databases often provide more current PTO trademark information. Below are some private online search companies.

- **Saegis** (www.thomson-thomson.com) Saegis is the most comprehensive trademark searching service and provides access to all Trademarkscan databases (state, federal, and international trademark databases), domain name databases, common law sources on the Internet, and access to newly filed United States federal trademark applications. Saegis also provides access to *Dialog* services.

- **Dialog** (www.dialog.com) *Dialog* provides access to *Trademarkscan* databases including state and federal registration and some international trademarks and provides common law searching of news databases.

- **Micropatent** (www.micropatent.com) Micropatent provides access to federal and state trademarks through its *MarkSearch Pro* and *MarkSearch Pro State* databases.

- **Trademark.com** (www.trademark.com) Trademark.com provides access to current federal and state trademark registration information.

- **Trademark Register** (www.trademarkregister.com) Trademark Register provides access to current federal registration information.

- **Marks on Line** (www.marksonline.com) Comprehensive trademark link site with listing of state and national trademark offices.

- **LEXIS/NEXIS** (www.lexis-nexis.com) LEXIS provides access to federal and state registrations and permits common law searching via NEXIS news services. The PTO utilizes NEXIS for its evaluations of descriptive and generic terms.

Many companies hire professional trademark searching companies such as Thomson & Thomson (www.thomson-thomson.com) to perform trademark searches. The cost is usually between two and three hundred dollars.

The name of your searcher and the sources searched (either by your searcher or by you if you did the search yourself) should be entered in the space provided.

The criteria for determining the extent to which you can prevent others from using your trademark, and whether it infringes on other existing trademarks, are discussed briefly in Chapter 1 of *Patent It Yourself*. You should consult a trademark attorney if you have any doubts about either or both of these points.

Once you decide on a trademark, you should file an application to register your trademark on the basis of your good faith intent to use it within the following six months. Then, when the trademark is actually used to market your invention across state lines, you can file an Amendment to Allege Use to get the trademark placed on the federal trademark register. If you are already using a trademark across state lines, your registration would be based on actual rather than intended use.

If you see that you won't be able to actually use the mark across state lines within the six-month period, you can obtain a six-month extension upon a showing of good cause. Four additional six-month extensions can also be obtained if you are able to convince the PTO that you still have a good faith intent to use the mark.

Under this system, you initially have several dates to keep track of:

- the date you first use your work within a state
- the date you file your trademark application to register on the basis of intended use
- the date you put the trademark into actual use across state lines, and
- the date you file your Amendment to Allege Use (or alternatively, your Statement of Use, if the PTO has by then issued the Notice of Allowance provisionally registering your mark).

You should also document when you first used the trademark in a foreign country, as this may be important should your trademark go international.

Your PTO registration provides notice throughout the U.S. that you claim ownership of and have the exclusive right to use the mark for the goods indicated in the registration. This notice can often make the difference between stopping other people from using your trademark and having to share use of the trademark with these later users. Also, it is much easier to collect damages for infringement of a registered trademark than an unregistered one. Use the space provided to document your federal registration efforts, including the date of registration, registration number, and registration classification name and number (all trademarks fall into

one or more specific classes of goods, each of which is assigned a number).

When your trademark is registered, you should note the date when you will need to file your declarations of continued use and incontestability (within the last year of the six-year period after your initial registration date). Thus, if you register your trademark with the PTO on July 1, 2000, you will want to file these declarations between July 1, 2005, and July 1, 2006. These declarations are statements that your trademark has been in continuous use for the preceding five-year period and that you qualify to have your trademark made incontestable (which immunizes it from attack on certain grounds). Failure to file the declaration of continued use will result in your trademark being cancelled. Assuming you are working with a trademark attorney, he or she will keep the date these declarations are due on the law firm calendar. You should also note the date you will want to initiate your ten-year renewal (about six months before the end of the ten-year period following your registration).

⚠ The protection and proper use of a trademark can be as commercially important as the underlying invention. We strongly recommend that you get a copy of *Trademark: Legal Care for Your Business and Product Name* by Attorney Stephen Elias (Nolo), and, if necessary, work with a trademark attorney on the matters covered in this chapter of *The Inventor's Notebook.*

H. Record of Contacts

Recommended Reading
Patent It Yourself, Chapter 1

It is extremely important that an inventor be able to identify each and every person and company who has been contacted about, or had access to, the invention. This information can prove to be very useful in the event of a dispute about:

- the inventor's diligence in building and testing the invention
- who should be considered the true inventor, or
- whether a confidentiality agreement has been violated.

 The Record of Contacts in Appendix II: Worksheets lets you keep notes of the people you have called, what you discussed the last time you spoke with them, and what their response was. This can be useful if you need to follow up on any calls.

Effective December 2000, every pending patent application will be published 18 months after its filing date. The only exception is if, at the time of filing, the applicant states that the application will not be filed abroad. In that case, once the patent issues on your invention, it becomes a matter of public record and is published in the *Official Gazette* (Patents). In both of these situations, publication terminates trade secret protection for the claimed invention. Prior to these publications, you are entitled to treat your invention as a trade secret and obtain court relief against those who improperly disclose your invention to others. Generally, a trade secret is any information which is maintained as confidential and which, because it is not generally known to competitors, provides its owner with a competitive edge. The basic method for preserving information as a trade secret is to limit those who have access to it, and require those who do have access to sign a confidentiality agreement. Blank agreement forms (called Proprietary Materials Agreements) are described in Chapter 1 and included in Appendix V: Tear-Out Forms.

By conscientiously entering all contacts in the Record of Contacts in Appendix II: Worksheets, and noting whether the person contacted has signed a confidentiality agreement, you will have all your contacts and trade secret protection information collected in one place for later reference.

I. Legal Protection Summary

Recommended Reading
Patent It Yourself, Chapter 7

An analysis of the relative advantages and disadvantages of the legal protection alternatives open to an inventor is provided in Chapter 7 of *Patent It Yourself.*

The Legal Protection Summary in Appendix II: Worksheets lets you keep track of which methods you have chosen to protect your invention.

This form can be very important when you go to market your invention. Most prospective buyers or developers will first want to know exactly what you've done to protect your right to exclusive use of the invention. By conscientiously keeping this list up-to-date, your record of protection will be instantly available to all who are interested. ∎

3

Marketing

Inventor's Commandment

You should try to market your invention as soon as you can after filing your patent application; don't wait until your patent issues. You should favor companies who are close to you and small in size.

If you want your invention to be successful, pursue commercial exploitation with all the energy which you can devote to it.

Never pay any money to any invention developer unless the developer can prove to you that it has a successful track record—that is, most of its clients have received more income in royalties than they have paid the developer in fees.

Simply put, this chapter is a preliminary guide to help you analyze the commercial potential of your invention and to help you keep track of your efforts to market it.

Once you invent something, you will naturally want to profit from it. This will involve coming up with a plan under which your invention can be produced and distributed to its ultimate users. To effectively get your invention "out there" you need to have a handle on what its strong and weak points are from both a marketing and manufacturing point of view (Section A). In addition, it's wise to consider how prospective manufacturers and users are likely to view your invention and to use this knowledge creatively as part of a plan to sell the idea of your new product (Section B). It's also important to understand general market trends in the particular area of your invention so that you will be prepared to tell interested marketers and manufacturers why your invention will be profitable given the costs to make it, the competition, and so on (Section C). In addition, you need to proceed in an organized manner to either seek potential manufacturers or distributors, or to accomplish these activities yourself. Sections E and F help you do this. Section G is an introduction to the Internet and how you can use the Internet to develop and promote your invention.

 The subject of marketing your invention to the public once it is manufactured is far beyond the scope of this book. If you plan to run the whole show, including the actual marketing of your invention, we suggest you consult one or more of the resources listed in Chapter 5, Help Beyond This Book.

A. Evaluation of Positive and Negative Factors of Invention

Recommended Reading
Patent it Yourself, Chapter 4

Inventor's Commandment

You should not spend significant time or money on your creation until you have thoroughly evaluated it for commercial potential, including considering all of its advantages and disadvantages.

Before you even prepare a patent application, you will obviously want to give serious consideration to whether your invention has commercial potential. For this reason, *Patent It Yourself* devotes an entire chapter to this question and provides an evaluation sheet to help you answer this key question. This same evaluation sheet has been included in Appendix II: Worksheets (Positive and Negative Factors Evaluation). Instructions from *Patent It Yourself* have been provided for your convenience.

1. The Positive and Negative Factors Test

Every invention, no matter how many positive factors it seems to have at first glance, inevitably has one or more significant negative ones. To evaluate the positive and negative factors objectively, carefully consider each on the list below. Using a Positive and Negative Factors Evaluation worksheet in Appendix II: Worksheets, assign a commercial value or disadvantage weight to each factor on a scale of 1 to 100, according to your best estimate.

For example, if an invention provides overwhelming cost savings in relation to its existing counterparts, assign an 80 or higher to the "Cost" factor (#1) in the positive column. If it requires a moderate capital expenditure to distribute, a 50 would be appropriate for this factor (#43), in the negative column.

The following balance scale analogy will help you understand the positive and negative factors evaluation process. Pretend the positive factors are stacked on one side of a balance scale and the negative factors are stacked on the other side, as indicated below.

If the positive factors strongly outweigh the negative, you can regard this as a "go" indication, i.e., the invention is commercially viable. Obviously this balance scale is just an analogy. It can't be used quantitatively because no one

has yet come up with a way to assign precise weights to the factors. Nevertheless, you'll find it of great help in evaluating the commercial prospects of your invention.

Before you actually take pen (or word processor) in hand and begin your evaluation, read through the following summary of positive and negative factors.

2. Positive Factors Affecting the Marketability of Your Invention

1. **Cost.** Is your invention cheaper to build or use than what is already used?
2. **Weight.** Is your invention lighter (or heavier) in weight than what is already known, and is such change in weight a benefit? For example, if you've invented a new automobile or airplane engine, a reduction in weight is a great benefit. But if you've invented a new ballast material, an increase in weight (provided it does not come at too great a cost in money or bulk) is a benefit.
3. **Size.** Is your invention smaller or larger in size or capacity than what is already known, and is such change in size a benefit?

4. **Safety/Health.** Is your invention safer or healthier to use than what is already known? Clearly there is a strong trend in government and industry to improve the safety and reduce the possible chances for injury or harm in most products and processes, and this trend has given birth to many new inventions. Often a greater increase in cost and weight can be tolerated if certain safety and health benefits accrue.

5. **Speed.** Is your invention able to do a job faster (or slower) than its previous counterpart, and is such change in speed a benefit?

6. **Ease of Use.** Is your invention easier (or harder) to use, or learn to use, than its previously known counterpart? For a combination lock, an increase in difficulty of use would be a benefit.

7. **Ease of Production.** Is your invention easier or cheaper (or harder or more expensive) to manufacture than previously known counterparts? Or can it be mass-produced, whereas previously known counterparts had to be made by hand? An example where making a device more difficult to manufacture would be of benefit is a credit card, which would be more difficult to forge if it were harder to make.

8. **Durability.** Does your invention last longer (or wear out sooner) than previously known counterparts? While built-in obsolescence is nothing to be admired, the stark economic reality is that many products, such as disposable razors, have earned their manufacturers millions by lasting for a shorter time than previously known counterparts.

9. **Repairability.** Is it easier to repair than previously known counterparts?

10. **Novelty.** Is your invention at all different from all previously known counterparts? Merely making an invention different may not appear to be an advantage per se, but it is usually a great advantage: It provides an alternate method or device for doing the job in case the first method or device ever encounters difficulties, for example, from government regulation, or in case the first device or method infringes a patent that you want to avoid infringing.

11. **Convenience/Social Benefit.** Does your invention make living easier or more convenient? Many inventions with a new function provide this advantage. Although you may question the ultimate wisdom and value of such gadgets as the electric knife, the remote-control TV, and the digital-readout clock, the reality remains that, in our relatively affluent society, millions of dollars have and are being made from devices that save labor and time (even though the time required to earn the after-tax money to buy the gadget is often greater than the time saved by using it). Then too, many new industries have been started by making an existing invention easier and more convenient to use. Henry Ford didn't invent the automobile; he just produced it in volume and made it convenient for the masses to use. Ditto for George Eastman with his camera. And in modern times, the two Steves (Jobs and Wozniak) did much the same for the computer.

12. **Reliability.** Is your invention apt to fail less or need repair less often than previously known devices?

13. **Ecology.** Does your invention make use of what previously were thought to be waste products? Does it reduce the use of limited natural resources? Does it produce fewer waste products, such as smoke, waste water, etc.? If so, you have an advantage which is very important and which should be emphasized strongly.

14. **Salability.** Is your invention easier to sell or market than existing counterparts?

15. **Appearance.** Does your invention provide a better-appearing design than existing counterparts?

16. **Viewability.** If your invention relates to eye use, does it present a brighter, clearer, or more viewable image? For example, a color TV with a brighter picture, or photochromic eyeglasses which automatically darken in sunlight are valuable inventions.

17. **Precision.** Does your invention operate or provide greater precision or more accuracy than existing counterparts?

18. **Noise.** Does your invention operate more quietly? Does it turn unpleasant noise into a more acceptable sound?

19. **Odor.** Does your invention emanate fewer or more unpleasant fumes or odors?

20. **Taste.** If your invention is edible or comes into contact with the taste buds (for example, a pill or a pipe stem), does it taste better? A foul taste (or smell) can also be an advantage, e.g., for poisons, to prevent ingestion by children, and for telephone cables, to deter chewing by rodents.

21. **Market Size.** Is there a larger market for your invention than for previously known devices? Because of climatic or legal restrictions, for example, certain inventions are only usable in small geographical areas. And because of economic factors, certain inventions may be limited to the relatively affluent. If your invention can obviate these restrictions, your potential market may be greatly increased, and this can be a significant advantage.

22. **Trend of Demand.** Is the trend of demand for your device increasing? Of course you should distinguish, if possible, between a trend and a fad. The first will provide a market for your invention while the second is likely to leave you high and dry unless you catch it in the beginning stages.

23. **Seasonal Demand.** Is your invention useful no matter what the season of the year? If so, it will have greater demand than a seasonal invention such as a sailboat.

24. **Difficulty of Market Penetration.** Is your device an improvement of a previously accepted device? If so, it will have an easier time penetrating the market than a device which provides a completely new function.

25. **Potential Competition.** Is your invention so simple, popular, or easy to manufacture that many imitators and copiers are likely to attempt to design around it, or break your patent as soon as it is brought out? Or is it a relatively complex, less popular, hard-to-manufacture device, which others would not be likely to produce in competition with you because of the large capital outlay required for tooling and production, etc.?

26. **Quality.** Does your invention produce or provide a higher quality output or result than existing counterparts? For example,

laser disks provide a much better audio quality than do phonorecords or magnetic tape.

27. **Excitement.** (The Neophile and the Conspicuous Consumer/Status Seeker). Almost all humans need some form of excitement in their lives: some obtain it by watching or participating in sports, others by travel, and still others by the purchase of new products, such as a 50-inch TV, a laser disk player, or a friendly household robot. Such purchasers can be called "neophiles" (lovers of the new); their excitement comes from having and showing off their new "toy." Purchasers of expensive products, like the Mercedes-Benz or a Rolex watch, commonly engage in what Thorsten Veblen has called "conspicuous consumption," and what we now call "status seeking." They enjoy showing off an expensive or unique item which they've acquired. Thus, if your invention can provide consumer excitement, either through sheer newness or through evidence of a costly purchase, it has a decided advantage.

28. **Markup.** If your invention is in an excitement category (i.e., if it is very different, novel, innovative, or luxurious), it can command a very high markup, a distinct selling advantage.

29. **Inferior Performance.** Yes, I'm serious! If your invention performs worse than comparable things which are already available, this can be a great advantage, if put to the proper use. Consider the 3M Company's fabulously successful Scotch® Post-It® note pads: Their novelty is simply that they have a strip of stickum which is inferior to known adhesives,

thus providing removable self-stick notes. Here the invention may not be so much the discovery of an inferior adhesive as the discovery of a new use for it.

30. **"Sexy" Packaging.** If your invention is or comes in a "sexy" package, or is adaptable to being sold in such a package, this can be a great advantage. Consider the Haines L'Eggs® stockings where the package (shaped like an egg) made the product!

31. **Miscellaneous/Obviation of Specific Disadvantages of Existing Devices.** This is a catchall to cover anything I may have

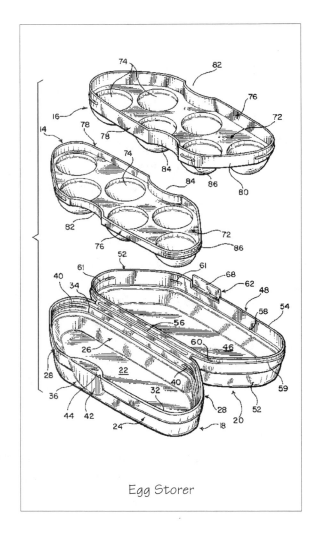

Egg Storer

missed in the previous categories. Often the specific disadvantages which your invention overcomes will be quite obvious; they should be included here, nonetheless.

32. **Long Life Cycle.** If your invention has a generally long life cycle, i.e., it can be made and sold for many years before it becomes obsolete, this is an obvious strong advantage which will justify a capital expenditure for tooling, a big ad campaign, etc.

33. **Related Product Addability.** If your invention will usher in a new product line, as did the computer, where many related products such as disk drives and printers can be added, this will be an important advantage with potentially enhanced profits.

34. **Satisfies Existing Need.** If your invention will satisfy an existing, recognized need, such as preventing drug abuse, or avoiding auto collisions, your marketing difficulties will be greatly reduced.

3. Negative Factors Likely to Affect the Marketability of Your Invention

Alas, every invention has one or more negative factors, even if the negative factor is merely the need to change—or design and produce—production equipment. We've seen inventions and developments that were better in every way than what already existed, but that were not used solely because the improvement did not justify the cost of replacing existing production equipment, or the cost associated with manufacturing and promoting the device.

The negative factors of your invention are generally more important and require more consideration than the positive factors, since if your invention fails, it will obviously be due to one or more of the negative factors. Since all the positive factors listed above can be disadvantages when viewed in reverse, they should be carefully considered, but will not be reproduced here. For example, consider Factor #23, Seasonal Demand. This will be a negative, rather than a positive factor if the invention is something like skis or a holiday decoration, which does have a seasonal demand, rather than an all-year-around one.

a. Negatives Are the Reverse of Positive Factors Listed Above

35. **Legality.** Does your invention fail to comply with, or will its use fail to comply with, existing laws, regulations, and product and manufacturing requirements? Or, are administrative approvals required? If your invention carries legal difficulties with it, its acceptance will be problematic no matter how great its positive advantages are. And if ecological or safety approvals are required (for example, for drugs and automobiles), this will be viewed as a distinct disadvantage by prospective buyers.

36. **Operability.** Is it likely to work, or will significant additional design or technical development be required to make it practicable and workable?

37. **Development.** Is the product already designed for the market, or will additional engineering, material selection, appearance work, etc., be required?

38. **Profitability.** Because of possible requirements for exotic materials, difficult

machining steps, great size, etc., is your invention likely to be difficult to sell at a profit?

39. **Obsolescence.** Is the field in which your invention is used likely to die out soon? If so, most manufacturers will not be willing to invest money in production facilities.

40. **Incompatibility.** Is your invention likely to be incompatible with existing patterns of use, customs, etc.?

41. **Product Liability Risk.** Is your invention in an area (such as drugs, firearms, contact sports, automobiles, etc.) where the risks of lawsuits against the manufacturer, due to product malfunction or injury from use, are likely to be greater than average?

42. **Market Dependence.** Is the sale of your invention dependent on a market for other goods, or is it useful in its own right? For example, an improved television tuner depends on the sale of televisions for its success, so that if the television market goes into a slump, the sales of your tuner certainly will fall also.

43. **Difficulty of Distribution.** Is your invention so large, fragile, perishable, etc., that it will be difficult or costly to distribute?

44. **Service Requirements.** Does your invention require frequent servicing and adjustment? If so, this is a distinct disadvantage. But consider the first commercial color TVs which, by any reasonable standard, were a service nightmare, but which made millions for their manufacturers.

45. **New Production Facilities Required.** Almost all inventions have this disadvantage. This is because the manufacture of anything new requires new tooling and production techniques.

46. **Inertia Must Be Overcome.** An example of a great invention that so far has failed because of user inertia is the Dvorak typewriter, which, although much faster and easier to use, was unable to overcome the awkward but entrenched Qwerty keyboard. If any invention is radically different, potential manufacturers, users, and sellers will usually manifest some inertia, despite the invention's value.

47. **Too Advanced Technically.** In the 60s, an inventor received a very broad patent on a laser pumped by a chemical reaction explosion. However, it was so advanced at the time that the technology behind it was not implemented until the "Star Wars" defense effort. Unfortunately, the patent expired in the meantime. The moral? Even if you have a great invention, make sure it can be commercially implemented within about 17 years.

48. **Substantial Learning Required.** If consumers will have to undergo substantial learning in order to use your invention, this is an obvious negative. An example: the early personal computers. On the other hand, some inventions, such as the automatically talking clock, make a task even easier to do and thus have an obvious strong advantage.

49. **Difficult to Promote.** If it will be difficult to promote your invention, e.g., because it's technically complex, has subtle advantages, or is very expensive, large, awkward, etc., you've got an obvious disadvantage.

50. **Lack of Market.** If no market already exists for your invention, you'll have to convince the public that they need it— that is, that you have a "product in search

of a market." While not a fatal flaw, and while this type of invention can be most profitable, you (or your licensee) will have to be prepared to expend substantial sums on promotion.

51. **Crowded Field.** If the field is already crowded, you'll have an uphill battle.

52. **Commodities.** If you've invented a new commodity—such as a better plastic, solvent, or grain—you'll face stiff price competition from the established, already streamlined standards.

53. **Combination Products.** If you've invented a "combination product"—that is, a product with two inventions that don't really groove together, like a stapler with a built-in beverage cup holder, people won't be beating a path to your door. On the other hand, the clock-radio was just the ticket.

54. **Entrenched Competition.** Despite its overwhelming advantages, Edison had a terrible time promoting his light bulb because the gas companies fought him bitterly.

55. **Instant Anachronism.** A clever inventor in Oakland, California, invented a wonderful dictionary indexing device which made it much faster to look up any word. However, he was unable to sell it to any dictionary publisher because the dictionary is being replaced by computerized devices. His clever invention was an "instant anachronism."

Complete the Positive and Negative Factors Evaluation form by assigning a weight to each listed factor, either in the positive or negative column. Also list and assign weights to any other factors you can think of which I've omitted. Then compute the sum of your positive and negative factors and determine the difference to come up with a rough idea of a net value for your invention. We suggest that you continue to pursue inventions with net values of 50 and up, that you direct your efforts elsewhere if your invention has a net value of less than 0, and that you make further critical evaluation of inventions with net values between 0 and 50.

 Again, we provide three tear-out copies of the Positive and Negative Factors Evaluation worksheet in Appendix II: Worksheets. The extra copies are in case you find others who can provide you with informed and impartial feedback on the commercial potential of your invention.

B. Potential User Survey

Recommended Reading
Patent It Yourself, Chapter 4

As part of your marketing efforts you will want to show that your invention is likely to be well accepted. One way to do this is a survey among likely users. This involves showing the invention to several such users, collecting their comments, entering them on the Potential User Survey in Appendix II: Worksheets, and (if convenient) having the users sign and date their comments. A good way to conduct this survey is to exhibit at local inventors' or new product fairs and showcases. Try a booth space in a local shopping mall. If your invention is patented, this type of survey can be done without having each person sign a Proprietary Materials Agreement. The important thing is to get as much feedback from the potential customers as possible. A professional marketing firm would charge quite a bit to provide this same information. The Potential User Survey permits this systematic documentation for later disclosure to investors or manufacturers.

The users should also sign a Proprietary Materials Agreement if you are maintaining your invention as a trade secret (at least until a patent issues). Tear-out copies of this agreement are contained in Appendix V: Tear-Out Forms.

C. Relevant Market Trends

To properly assess your invention's commercial potential, it's wise to carefully consider what existing trends, if any, will affect its acceptance in the marketplace. As mentioned above, a clever inventor in Oakland, California, invented a wonderful dictionary indexing device which made it much faster to look up any word. However, he was unable to sell it to any dictionary publisher because the dictionary was being replaced by computerized devices. His clever invention was an instant anachronism. Obviously, with some inventions, such as a dictionary indexing device, you have little choice but to swim against the commercial stream, unless of course you decide that the current is so swift that you're better off putting the invention aside in favor of something else.

We have designed three forms to document (at least preliminarily) the trends which bear on the marketability of your invention. These forms can be particularly essential if you plan to seek venture capital or a business partner. It also, of course, is the basis of any intelligent marketing strategy. When a potential investor or partner says, "Tell me exactly how this thing will make money," the more persuasive your analysis of market trends, the better your chance of successfully completing the transaction.

Let's say you go back to work and invent a new type of translucent bowling ball which contains holographic images that change as the ball rolls. The images could be attractive patterns, pictures of film or music celebrities, etc. If you want to sell this idea to a large manufacturer of related products, such as AMF or Brunswick, there is probably no point for you to spend time and money on an extensive market survey; they already know more about this area than you could ever hope to. If, on the other hand, you are seeking capital from someone who is not an expert in the field, you are going to have to convince him that the combination of bowling balls and holographic images is likely to be a hot item, at least in some areas of the country or among certain age groups. Simply put, will your bowling ball "play in Peoria"?

To answer this question for your invention, you will want to find data that tells you about:

- previous and forecasted buying patterns for related or competing products in your targeted marketing areas, and
- the projected size and buying power of the population groups of your most likely customers.

Where do you find this type of information? There are several specialized reference sources, available in large public libraries, which will provide you with enough information to at least partially answer these types of questions. Chief among these reference sources are:

- *Predicasts Forecasts.* This service abstracts information in newspapers, business magazines, trade journals, and government reports that deals with market data, financial data, capacities, production, product development, trade, technology, and forecasts. It is published quarterly by Predicasts.
- *U.S. Industrial Outlook.* This service contains the prospects for over 350 manufacturing and service industries. It is published by the U.S. Department of Commerce.
- *Statistical Reference Index.* This publication indexes and abstracts American statistical publications from private organizations and government sources. It is published by the Congressional Information Service (CIS) and is especially useful for obtaining key demographic information.
- *American Statistical Index.* This service indexes and abstracts statistical information published by the U.S. government. It is also useful for amassing demographic information.
- *Standard and Poor's Index.* This publication is published by Standard and Poor's Corporation and is useful for obtaining marketing information as it relates to companies.
- *Hine's Directory of Published Market Research.* This publication is a valuable directory to market research which has been carried out for other products and services.

Each of these publications contains detailed instructions on how to use it; reference librarians can also be quite helpful.

Vast amounts of market research information are available online, some for a fee and some for free. Fee-based services such as LEXIS/ NEXIS (www.lexis-nexis.com/business/), Dialog (www.dialog.com), and IQUEST (www.iquest. com) provide substantial databases of company facts and information. A great deal of information is available for free through business directories and databases online at small business sites such as Yahoo (http://dir.yahoo.com/Business_ and_Economy/Small_Business_Information/) or Entrepreneur.com (www.entrepreneur.com).

A third alternative is to have someone else search the databases for you. Below is a listing of some information searching companies:

- Research on Demand (www.researchondemand.com/)
- Business Research Services (http:// www.marketingresearch.com/ contact.htm)
- Knowledge Now (www.know-now.com/ business_research.htm)
- Berlinerspy (http://berlinerspy.com/)
- Infoscope (www.infoscope.com).

These services provide marketing and research reports usually for several hundred dollars or more. While this may seem like a lot of money, the search materials are usually worth the price and the results will enhance your ability to convince others to produce or invest in your invention. You can locate information searching companies on the Internet using search terms such as "business research services."

⚠ Before you spend a lot of money for a search conducted by others, ask for and check references. The sources you use should not only be reputable but should be independently verifiable by anyone from whom you are seeking funds.

D. How to Record Relevant Marketing Trend Data From These Types of Sources

Appendix II: Worksheets contains three forms to record your research on relevant market trends. They are:

- Regional Buying Patterns of Related Products
- Predictions for Targeted Buying Groups
- Conclusions Regarding Market Trends.

There are three copies of each form to provide adequate room for more extensive surveys, or for the possibility of subsequent surveys for improved versions of your invention.

On the Regional Buying Patterns of Related Products form you should enter information you have located for sales of related products by geographical region. Taking our bowling ball example, related products could be (A) bowling balls, (B) holograms, (C) high-tech recreation products, (D) celebrity paraphernalia, and (E) bowling lanes. The relevant geographic regions would most likely begin with your local area and proceed to state or regional comparisons, national surveys, and even, if appropriate, international markets.

The Predictions for Targeted Buying Groups form allows you to enter demographic information gleaned from your research. First, identify the potential purchaser groups that you think will account for the largest number of sales by Age, Sex, and Other. Then, for each group, look at their numbers as a percentage of the overall population in three promising market areas (regions). Also, take a look at the average disposable income of each group by

Regional Buying Patterns of Related Products

	Product Name	Source of Information	Sales for Last Year Surveyed	Projected Sales
Region:	_____			
Product A	_____	_____	_____	_____
Product B	_____	_____	_____	_____
Product C	_____	_____	_____	_____
Product D	_____	_____	_____	_____
Product E	_____	_____	_____	_____

Regional Buying Patterns of Related Products

Predictions for Targeted Buying Groups

	Potential Purchasers	Age	Sex	Other	Predicted % of Sales
Group 1	_____	____	____	_____	_____
Group 2	_____	____	____	_____	_____
Group 3	_____	____	____	_____	_____

Source of Information	Last Year Surveyed	Projected

GROUP 1

% of Population

Region 1	_____	_____	_____
Region 2	_____	_____	_____
Region 3	_____	_____	_____

Disposable Income

Region 1	_____	_____	_____
Region 2	_____	_____	_____
Region 3	_____	_____	_____

Predictions for Targeted Buying Groups

region. For example, Group 1 may be those aged 13–18 of both sexes who bowl, while Group 2 may be identified in the "Other" category as owners of bowling alleys.

For Group 1, under "% of Population," you would want to record both the present and predicted percentage of the entire population for this group in each region. This category would be irrelevant for Group 2, since the percentage of bowling alley owners is negligible. Under "Disposable Income," you may want to record some data about the relative wealth of teenagers —this would bear on how much they have to spend on recreation. Your Group 2 data in this area might focus on such items as how much owners of bowling alleys spend annually replacing old balls and how much is spent on advertising to get more young people into bowling.

The Conclusions Regarding Marketing Trends form asks you to use the data entered in the first two parts to draw some conclusions about the market trends affecting your product. To see how this is done, let's again return to our example of the holographic bowling ball. You may have found that:

- the numbers of young people in the age groups you hope to sell your invention to are projected to decrease
- the relative buying power of these young people is rapidly rising relative to the population as a whole
- the sales of bowling balls and accessories are fairly steady
- money spent on teen idol "essentials" and futuristic toys is steadily climbing, and
- young people bowl in much larger numbers in the Southeast than the Midwest.

While the first finding is essentially negative from a marketability standpoint, the other findings are essentially positive. Make a written record of both the positive and negative results of your survey and how they may influence your marketing strategy. In your presentation to a venture capital source, you should point out the increase in disposable income and interest in holograms and stars, and that you have decided to introduce your new sensation in the Southeast with the idea of creating a fad that will bring more young people into bowling alleys across the country. If you can back up this marketing approach with some solid information, you have a much better chance of being listened to.

E. Manufacturer/ Distributor Evaluation

Recommended Reading
Patent It Yourself, Chapter 11

The Inventor's Decision Chart in the Introduction asks you to decide whether you want to manufacture your invention yourself, and if so, whether you also plan to handle its distribution. The Manufacturer/Distributor Evaluation forms in Appendix II: Worksheets help you organize the facts on which these decisions should ultimately be based.

F. Choosing the Right Company and Reaching the Decision Maker

If you decide to have someone else manufacture your invention, you need to decide which companies to approach. To do so efficiently:

- Choose companies that operate in your field, or in a related one.
- Consider size—depending on your product, you may want to deal with a small entrepreneurial outfit, or a multinational corporation.
- Consider location—companies with headquarters close to you are usually easier to approach.
- Consider company attitudes and products—do you like the company and its products?
- Consider marketing—if your product will require a good deal of consumer education to succeed (e.g., a machine that makes a cross between yogurt and peanut butter), will the company commit to a big advertising push or other long-term marketing technique that focuses on consumer education?

Companies can be researched in the same manner as products and services (see Section C above), either through the following written resources or in computer databases.

- *Thomas Register of American Manufacturers*

- *Dun and Bradstreet's Million Dollar Directory*
- *Standard and Poor's Index*
- *MacRae's Verified Directory of Manufacturers' Representatives*
- *Encyclopedia of Associations* (which alerts you to the trade associations and journals that relate your invention)
- *Science Citation Index* (for scientific/ technical information)
- *Business Periodical Index* (for business and finance information).

You can also locate information about companies using online business directories. There are various general business directories on the Internet and your search engine should be capable of finding them. One website that may be helpful is BigYellow (www.bigyellow.com), the NYNEX business directory. It enables you to search by business category, name, street address, state, or zip code. Most online services have general business directories that perform the same functions. On America Online, consult the American Business Information (ABI) forum and you can locate companies based on name or industry.

Also helpful are database companies (sometimes known as mailing list or sales leads companies) that compile listings of millions of businesses. For a fee they will supply you with a listing of all the companies within a particular industry. For example, if you had invented a device that improves air circulation in motor homes, a database company could supply you with a printed mailing list for 128 motor home manufacturers. You can find database companies in your local Yellow Pages, usually listed under "Mailing Lists." For an example of one such company located on the Internet, check out InfoUsa (www.infousa.com).

SIC Codes

Corporations that manufacture products utilize a system known as the Standard Industrial Classification Code (SIC). The SIC is a four-digit number created by the Department of Commerce and is used to classify a business by the type of work it does. For example, if you invented a product to be worn while handling explosives, you might review companies classified as 1795, which is the code for the Wrecking and Demolition Industry. If you invented a timer for video cameras, you would check companies classified as 3651 for Video Equipment and Household Audio. The SIC is helpful when searching, since most corporate directories, whether in print, digital, or online form, include an index of SIC codes.

Information about any given company can also be obtained through a professional search company, as with the marketing information discussed in Section C above.

You are most likely to do well with smaller companies near enough to you so that you would have no difficulty making a visit to personally demonstrate the advantages of your invention. Choose a company that is in a similar product line and has the marketing, distribution, and advertising appropriate to sell your item. It is important to target companies that are doing well financially; even the simplest of ideas will require a substantial investment to bring to market.

The president of the company is who you must reach, if at all possible. He knows where he wants the company to go and he knows if the resources are available to get there. Try phoning before or after normal business hours—these guys are in the office ten or more hours a day, if you are lucky enough to catch them in town. Give a brief listing of the advantages of your product and ask if you can send them your Proprietary Materials Agreement. If you have difficulty getting to the president, obtain an Annual Report and try contacting members of the Board of Directors or past or retired presidents.

The universal key to making a good living as an inventor is perseverance, but it doesn't hurt to work smart. For instance, when seeking out an appropriate company for your invention, you might be wise to attend one or two trade shows. The contacts you can make at these types of gatherings can get more done for you than weeks in a library.

Record the results of your company research on the Choosing the Right Company worksheet in Appendix II: Worksheets.

G. Using the Internet to Develop and Promote Your Invention

As an inventor, you know that creativity is only part of what it takes to be successful. Technical, marketing, and legal knowledge, sources of financing, collaborators, or licensees are also needed to get the most for your efforts. The following websites have been selected specifically as starting points for inventors to explore for purposes of developing and promoting your invention. Remember, the Web is constantly changing with websites coming and going every minute of every day. Additional sites and resources are provided in Appendix C.

- **U. S. Patent and Trademark Office** (www.uspto.gov)—includes extensive information on profiting from patents in its Independent Inventor Resources.
- **U.S. Small Business Administration** (www.sba.gov)—thorough online guide for entrepreneurs and small companies.
- **The Institute of Management and Administration** (www.ioma.com)—a super site for business managers.
- **Patent Law Links** (www.patentlawlinks.com) provides links to everything "patent" on the Internet.
- **The Patent Café** (www.patentcafe.com)— exhaustive links to patent marketing and business sites. ■

4

Financing

This chapter of *The Inventor's Notebook* helps you organize your search for funds to build and test, manufacture, and distribute your invention. First you need to create a budget so that you can arrive at several estimates of how much capital you are likely to need in the course of getting your invention out of your head and into the marketplace. The Checklist for Selling Invention/Seeking Capital walks you through the steps you should take before trying to sell the invention or before seeking funding to market it yourself. Finally, the Funding Sources and Results helps you to keep track of your funding and/or sales efforts.

A. Determination of Funds Needed

Recommended Reading
Pratt's Guide to Venture Capital Sources by Stanley E. Pratt (Venture Economics Inc., annual edition)

Some inventors have the luxury of being able to invent without worrying about who will pick up the tab. Most of us, however, must keep a close eye on our budgets. The Budget worksheet allows you to record cost estimates of your activities before initiating the building, testing, production, and marketing phases of your invention. The Budget contains headings which prompt you to categorize the expenses appropriate to your invention. This means that you may be using some parts of the Budget worksheet and not others. Because there is usually a range of possibilities for costs, we provide space for a high, low, and middle estimate. The documentation called for in this section will help you design an appropriate business plan for your invention to show to persons or organizations you are seeking capital from.

 We include three copies of the budget form in Appendix II: Worksheets. If you modify your invention after making one budget, you can fill out another sheet for the new version.

B. Checklist for Selling Invention/Seeking Capital

Recommended Reading
Patent It Yourself, Chapter 11

A number of important steps must be taken before you are ready to present your invention to the world. The Checklist for Selling Invention/Seeking Capital in Appendix II: Worksheets provides space for you to keep track of these steps so that you can be equipped to make a thoroughly businesslike presentation when you approach potential buyers. The first page is a checklist of steps necessary to prepare you for the presentation of your invention to potential purchasers or investors. The second page will help you focus on the essential points you want to cover, prepare responses to any possible questions, and reflect on the results of a practice presentation (we recommend that you practice your presentation with an associate or friend prior to the real thing). Your entries here should be brief notes to serve as reminders rather than full-blown essays.

Two Additional Suggestions

One of the most surefire ways to raise money for a new idea is to get a significant number of purchase orders in hand. A good way to do this is to exhibit in one of the major trade shows in your product's industry. If you are going to do this, you should have your homework done—samples that work and have a professional finish, the proper legal protection for your idea, sales literature, attractive packaging, an awareness of who the buyers are for the major accounts you want to land, and the ability to deliver on the orders. If this event goes well, you will not only be able to obtain the financing you need—you may also receive offers from large companies to buy the rights to your invention.

Another way to substantiate the demand for your invention/product, and thereby increase the interest of investors, is from the responses generated by a press release in a national publication. Many magazines print news about new inventions or products. This does not cost you a thing other than the preparation of the materials you submit. Write to the individual publications for their guidelines on the preparation of press releases. Make sure that any photos you submit are of professional quality.

C. Funding Sources and Results

 Recommended Reading
How to Write a Business Plan, Chapter 3

As you know, funding can come from many different sources (with their attendant pluses and minuses), and it is likely to take more than one try to obtain the money you need. Make a record of those you contact and their response on the Funding Sources and Results in Appendix II: Worksheets. If their reply is positive, how much money they committed; if negative, why they turned you down. This will give you a current assessment of how much more you need to ask for, and may prompt you to make changes in your method of presentation. ■

5

Help Beyond This Book

Throughout this notebook we have suggested specific outside readings for each section. This part is designed to help you find additional resources that can extend your understanding of issues addressed in this book and help you answer questions and address issues not covered by this book.

In Section A, we direct you to sources for more information for inventors. In Section B, we provide additional resources on patents and intellectual property law.

A. Inventor Resources

The following is a list of inventor resources, including organizations, bookstores, and websites with special information on patents and other intellectual property issues.

- **Inventor's Bookstore** (www.inventorhelp.com). The Inventor's Bookstore offers condensed reports and other guidance for inventors.

- **Inventors' Digest** (www.inventorsdigest.com). The *Inventors' Digest* and its accompanying website publish information for independent inventors at a subscription rate of $27/year for six issues. It includes articles on new inventions, licensing and marketing, and advertisements from reputable inventor promotion companies.

- **National Inventor Fraud Center** (www.inventorfraud.com). This organization reports on fraud by invention marketing companies.

- **National Technology Transfer Center (NTTC)** (www.nttc.edu). The NTTC at Wheeling Jesuit University helps entrepreneurs and companies looking to access federally funded research and development activity at American universities. Write to 316 Washington Avenue, Wheeling, WV 26003. Phone: 800-678-6882. Fax: 304-243-4388. Email: technology@nttc.edu.

- **Patent It Yourself** (www.patentityourself.com). Patent information and updates for David Pressman's *Patent It Yourself* (Nolo).

- **PTO Independent Inventor Resources** (www.uspto.gov/web/offices/com/iip/indextxt.htm). In 1999, the PTO established a new office aimed at providing services and support to independent inventors. This office is expected to eventually offer seminars and expanded educational opportunities for inventors. Phone: 800-PTO-9199 or 703-308-HELP.

- **Ronald J. Riley's Inventor Resources** (www.inventored.org). This website provides comprehensive links and advice for inventors.

- **The Patent Cafe** (www.patentcafe.com). An inventor resource maintained by inventor and entrepreneur Andy Gibbs. It lists inventor organizations and related links and provides information on starting an inventor organization.

- **Source Translation and Optimization Patent Website** (www.bustpatents.com). A source of information on questionable patents and patent practices by one of the PTO's most vocal critics. Also offers a free newsletter.

- **United Inventors Association (UIA)** (www.uiausa.org). A national inventor's organization. Write to P.O. Box 23447, Rochester, NY 14692-3347. Phone: 716-359-9310. Fax: 716-359-1132. Email: UIAUSA@aol.com.

B. Patent and Intellectual Property Resources

Provided below are some additional sources of information on patent and intellectual property law. Many of these sources are accessible through the Internet.

1. Nolo Books on Intellectual Property

There is a world of intellectual property law beyond patents. If you are interested in understanding other principles of intellectual property law that may apply to your invention, Nolo.com, the publisher of this book, also publishes a number of other titles on intellectual property, including:

- *Copyright Your Software* by attorney Stephen Fishman.
- *Patent It Yourself* by attorney David Pressman.
- *Nolo's Patents for Beginners* by attorney Richard Stim
- *Patent, Copyright and Trademark: A Desk Reference to Intellectual Property Law* by attorney Stephen Elias
- *Software Development: A Legal Guide* by attorney Stephen Fishman
- *The Copyright Handbook* by attorney Stephen Fishman
- *The Public Domain* by attorney Stephen Fishman
- *Trademark: Legal Care for Your Business and Product Name* by attorneys Kate McGrath and Stephen Elias
- *How to Make Patent Drawings Yourself* by Patent Agent Jack Lo and attorney David Pressman

- *Patent Searching Made Easy* by David Hitchcock.

2. Additional Intellectual Property Resources

- **U.S. Copyright Office** (http://www.loc.gov/copyright). The Copyright Office has numerous circulars, kits, and other publications that can help you, including one on searching copyright records. These publications and application forms can be obtained by writing to the Copyright Office at Publications Section, LM-455, Copyright Office, Library of Congress, Washington, DC 20559. Most Copyright Office publications can be downloaded at www.loc.gov/copyright. Frequently requested circulars and announcements are also available via the Copyright Office's fax-on-demand telephone line at 202-707-9100.
- **Fedlaw** (http://fedlaw.gsa.gov/). Fedlaw is a source of federal law links with a thorough collection of intellectual property statutes, case law, and readings.
- **Government Printing Office** (www.access.gpo.gov/#info). The Government Printing Office website is a searchable source for U.S. Code of Federal Regulations, *Congressional Record,* and other Government Printing Office products and information.
- **Intellectual Property Mall** (www.ipmall.fplc.edu). Franklin Pierce Law Center's Intellectual Mall provides IP links and information.
- **Internet Patent News Service** (www.bustpatents.com). The Internet

Patent News Service is a source for patent news, information about searching, and patent documents.

- **Legal Information Institute** (http://lii.law. cornell.edu). The Legal Information Institute provides intellectual property links and downloadable copies of statutes and cases.

- **Patent It Yourself** (www.patentityourself.com). This website provides information regarding the patent application process.

- **U.S. Patent & Trademark Office (PTO): Patent Information** (www.uspto.gov). The PTO website offers a number of informational pamphlets. There is also an alphabetical and geographical listing of patent attorneys and agents registered to practice before the PTO ("Directory of Registered Patent Attorneys and Agents Arranged by States and Countries"). The PTO also has an online searchable database of patent abstracts (short summaries of patents). For purposes of patent searching, this database is an excellent and inexpensive first step in the searching procedure. Most patent forms can be downloaded from the PTO website as well as many important publications, including *General Information About Patents, Manual of Patent Examining Procedures, Examination Guidelines for Computer-Related Inventions,* and *Disclosure Document Program.* A PTO products and services catalog is also available. Phone: 800-PTO-9199.

- **Trade Secrets Home Page** (www.execpc.com/~mhallign). The website includes explanations of trade secret law online and current trade secret news.

- **U.S. Patent & Trademark Office (PTO): Trademark Information.** Trademarks are examined and registered by a division of the PTO. *General Information About Trademarks,* an introductory pamphlet about trademarks, and other information about the operations of the Patent and Trademark Office, is available from the Superintendent of Documents, Government Printing Office, Washington, DC 20402, or from the PTO's website at www.uspto.gov. This site also includes the relevant applications and trademark office forms. You can also write to the Commissioner for Trademarks, 2900 Crystal Drive, Arlington, VA 22202-3515.

- **U.S. Code** (http://uscode.house.gov/usc.htm). This website is a source for the United States Code, which includes copyright, trademark, and patent laws.

- **Yahoo Intellectual Property Directory** (www.yahoo.com/Government/Law/ Intellectual_Property). The Yahoo Intellectual Property Directory is a thorough listing of intellectual property resources on the Internet.

- ***The PCT Applicant's Guide,*** a brochure on how to utilize the PCT, is available for free from the PCT Department of the U.S. Patent & Trademark Office. PCT information and software for facilitating completion of the PCT forms is available through the PCT's website (www.wipo.int). It is also available from the World Intellectual Property Organization (WIPO), Post Office Box 18, 1211 Geneva 20, Switzerland, and on the PCT's website (www.wipo.int).

Recommended Reading

Nolo's website (www.nolo.com) also offers an extensive Legal Encyclopedia that includes a section on intellectual property. You'll find answers to frequently asked questions about patents, copyrights, trademarks, and other related topics, as well as sample chapters of Nolo books and a wide range of articles. Simply click "Legal Encyclopedia" and then "Patent, Copyright & Trademark." ■

I

Notebook

Record of Conception of Invention

Title of invention:

INTERNATIONAL LANGUAGES TRANSLATOR AND COMMUNICATOR.

Circumstances of conception:

ON THE EVENING OF THIS DAY, OCTOBE, 26, 2004 ARROUND 7:30 P.M. I JAVIER SALVADOR HERNANDEZ, ATTENDING THE CLASS CIS-041 INTRODUCTION TO COMPUTERS. INFORMATION SYSTEMS, IN THE CLASSROOM. T-203 LOCATED ON THE SECOND FLOOR OF THE TECHNOLOGY CENTER. AT SAN JOSE CITY COLLEGE. WHICH ADDRESS IS 2100 MOORPARK AVE. SAN JOSE CA. 95128 THE INTRUCTOR OF THE CLASS, MY CLASSMATES AND MYSELF, WERE. DISCUSSING ABOUT DIFFERENT IMPUT AND OUTPUT DEVICES THAT CAN BE USED IN CONJUNTION WITH THE COMPUTER, WHEN SUDDENLY I HAD A "FLASH OF GENIUS" OR ~~STO~~ A BRAIN STORM. AND CAME OUT WITH THE "IDEA" OF A NEW INVENTION, WHICH AT THE MOMENT I CALLED IT, LANGUAGE. TRANSLATOR AND COMMUNICATOR. THE INSTRUCTOR AND ALL THE CLASSMATES INMEDIATELY AGREED THAT WAS A VERY GOOD. IDEA. THAT IS WY I'M RECORDING ALL THIS INFORMATION.

Purpose or problem solved:

~~WHI~~ WITH THE CREATION OF THIS NEW DEVICE, ANY PERSON, SPEAKING ANY LANGUAGE, CAN TRAVEL TO ANY PART OF THE WORLD, SPEAK ON THEIR OWN LANGUAGE TO THE DEVICE AND THE. DEVICE USING VOICE RECOGNITION TECHNOLOGY, TRANSLATES ON THE. SELECTED LANGUAGE. INSTANTENUOUSLY, THIS WAY THE PROBLEM OF COMMUNICATING WHEN TRAVELING TO DIFFERENT CONTRIES AND NOT KNOWING HOW TO SPEAK ALL THOSE LANGUAGES, CAN BE EASELY SOLVED ~~WHI9~~ WITH THIS NEW INVENTION. ALSO CAN BE ADDED AN EXTENSIVE USE TRANSCATING ALL THE DIFFERENT DIALECTS THAT PEOPLE SPEAK IN ANY COUNTRY TO THE NATIONAL LANGUAGE. AND FACILITATE THE COMMUNICATION.

Invented by: ___JAVIER SALVADOR HERNANDEZ.___ Date: __10-27-04__

Invented by: _____ Date: _____

The above confidential information is witnessed and understood by:

_____ Date: _____

_____ Date: _____

Record of Conception of Invention

Description and operation:

THIS A NEW DEVICE OR ELECTRONIC GADGET, EQUIPPED WITH HIGH DEFINITION, SPEACH INDEPENDENT VOICE RECOGNITION TECHNOLOGY PROGRAM. ALSO IS EQUIPPED WITH A BUILT-IN MICROPHONE OR A COMBINATION OF EARPHONES AND MICROPHONE THAT WHICH CAN BE CONNECTED TO THE DIVICE. ALSO IS EQUIPPED WITH A BUILTINE SPEACKER SO WHEN YOU SPEACK ON YOUR OWN LANGUAGE THROUGH THE BUILT IN MICROPHONE THE PERSON, OR GROUP CAN HEAR THE TRANSLATION OF WHAT YOU SAID, ON THEIR OWN LANGUAGE THROUGH THE SPEACKER. AND SINCE THEY HAVE THE SAME DIVICE THE ONLY THING THEY HAVE TO DO IS REVERSE THE PROCESS THEN YOU CAN HEAR WHEREVER THEY SAID ON YOUR OWN LANGUAGE. ANOTHER ALTERNATIVE THAT CAN BE ADDED IN THE FUTURE TO THE DIVICE IS OTHER CONNECTION FOR ANOTHER. COMBO MICROPHONE AND EARPHONE SET SO THE OTHER PERSON CAN USE IT SPEAKING ON HIS OWN LANGUAGE. THE DIVICE MAKES THE INSTANT TRANSLATION WHICH YOU ARE GOING TO TEA LISTEN ON YOUR OWN LANGUAGE. THIS WAY YOU CAN HAVE A CONVERSATION WITH THIS PERSON.

THIS DIVICE ON THE BASSIC STAGE CAN BE USE FOR TWO LANGUAGES AT A TIME LIKE ENGLISH-CHINESE OR ENGLISH-RUSSIAN. AND WHEN FULLY DEVELOPED, CAN BE USED FOR MULTILANGUAGES. LIKE INGLISH TO CHINESE, FRENCH, RUSSIAN, ITALIAN, PORTUGUESE, SPANISH, HINDU ETC. AND VICEVERSA FROM ALL THIS LANGUAGES TO INGLISH. THIS DEVICE IS ALSO EQUIPED WITH WIRELESS CONNECTION TO CONNECT THROUGH THE INTERNET TO A MAIN FRAME COMPUTER.

Invented by: __JAVIER SALVADOR HERNANDEZ__   Date: __10-27-04__

Invented by: _____   Date: _____

The above confidential information is witnessed and understood by:

_____   Date: _____

_____   Date: _____

Record of Conception of Invention

Description and operation:

WHERE ALL PROGRAMS FOR THE TRANSLATION AND COMMUNICATION OF ALL THE LANGUAGES AND DIALECTS ARE GOING TO BE STORED. SO ANY BODY CAN REQUEST THE SERVICE FROM ANY PART OF THE WORLD. THE SERVICE CAN BE USED IN CONJUNCTION WHITH ANE OF THE EXISTING GADGETS. LIKE A DESKTOP COMPUTER, P.D.A. NOTEBOOK, SMART PHONE. OR ANY OTHER MOBIL GADGET. BUT A NEW CONCEPT OR A NEW DIVICE IS PREEFERIBLE BECOUSE IS GOING TO BE EQUIPED WITH ALL THE CONNECTIONS NECESARY AND THE SELECTORS OF THE LANGUAGES NEED IT TO FACILITATE THE INSTANT TRANSLATION AND COMMUNICATION

Invented by: _____ Date: _____

Invented by: _____ Date: _____

The above confidential information is witnessed and understood by:

_____ Date: _____

_____ Date: _____

Record of Conception of Invention

Description and operation:

_____

_____

_____

_____

_____

_____

_____

_____

_____

_____

_____

_____

_____

_____

_____

_____

_____

_____

_____

_____

_____

_____

_____

_____

_____

_____

_____

_____

_____

_____

_____

Invented by: _____ Date: _____

Invented by: _____ Date: _____

The above confidential information is witnessed and understood by:

_____ Date: _____

_____ Date: _____

Record of Conception of Invention

Drawing:

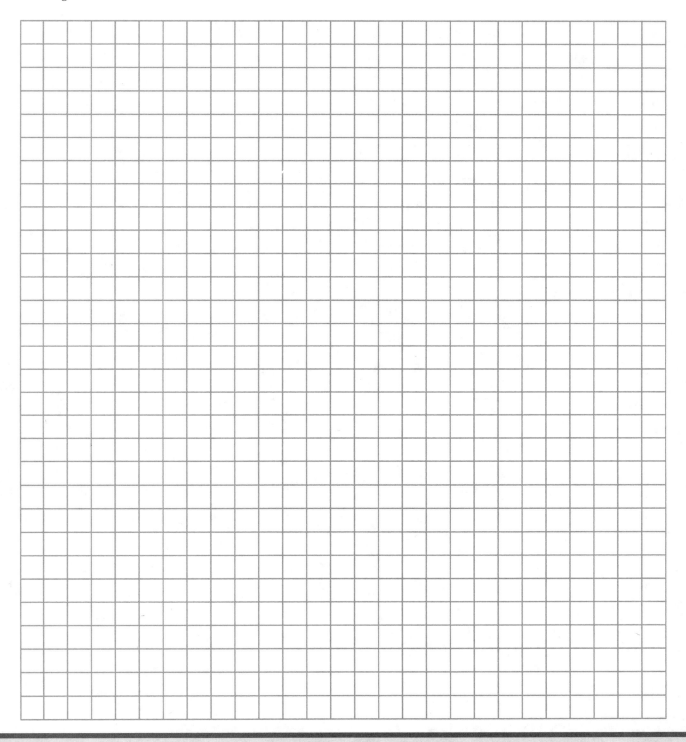

Invented by: _____ Date: _____

Invented by: _____ Date: _____

The above confidential information is witnessed and understood by:

_____ Date: _____

_____ Date: _____

Record of Conception of Invention

Drawing:

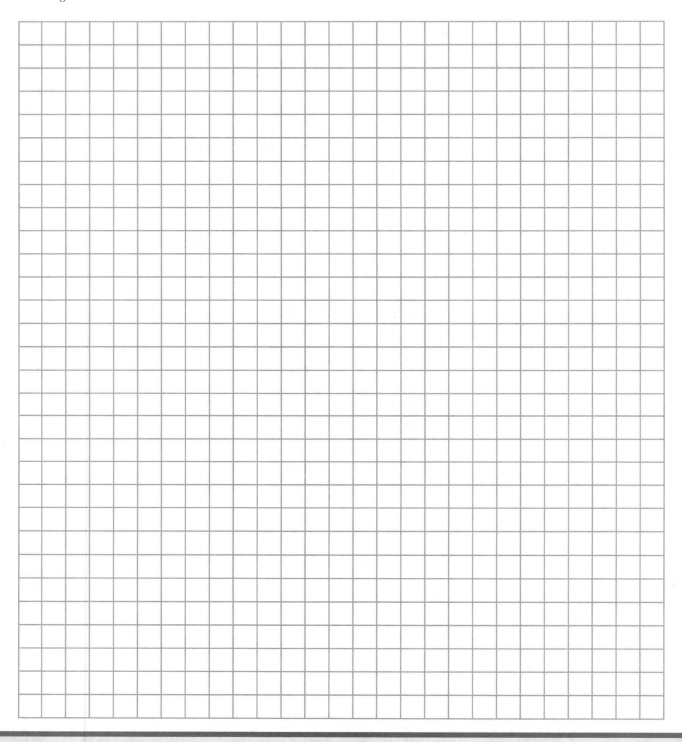

Invented by: _____ Date: _____

Invented by: _____ Date: _____

The above confidential information is witnessed and understood by:

_____ Date: _____

_____ Date: _____

Record of Conception of Invention

Drawing:

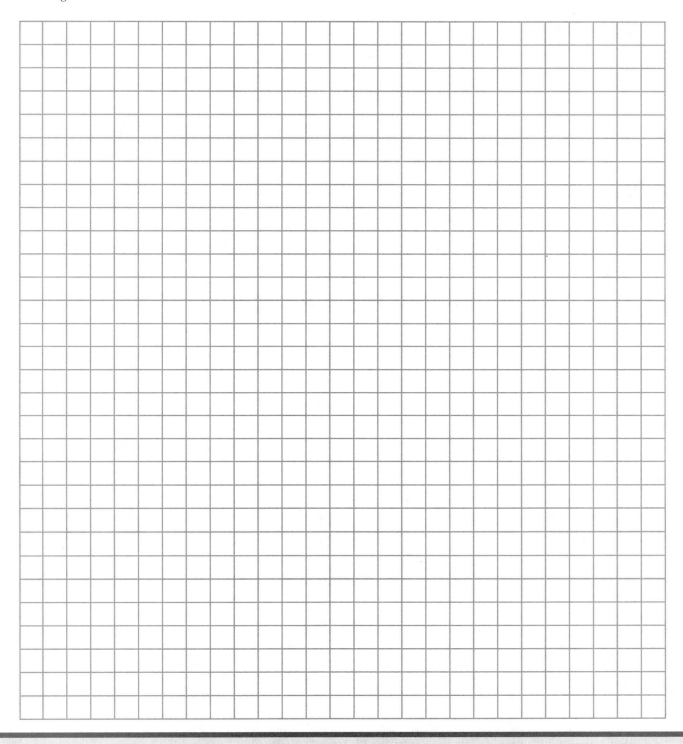

Invented by: _____   Date: _____

Invented by: _____   Date: _____

The above confidential information is witnessed and understood by:

_____   Date: _____

_____   Date: _____

Record of Conception of Invention

Drawing:

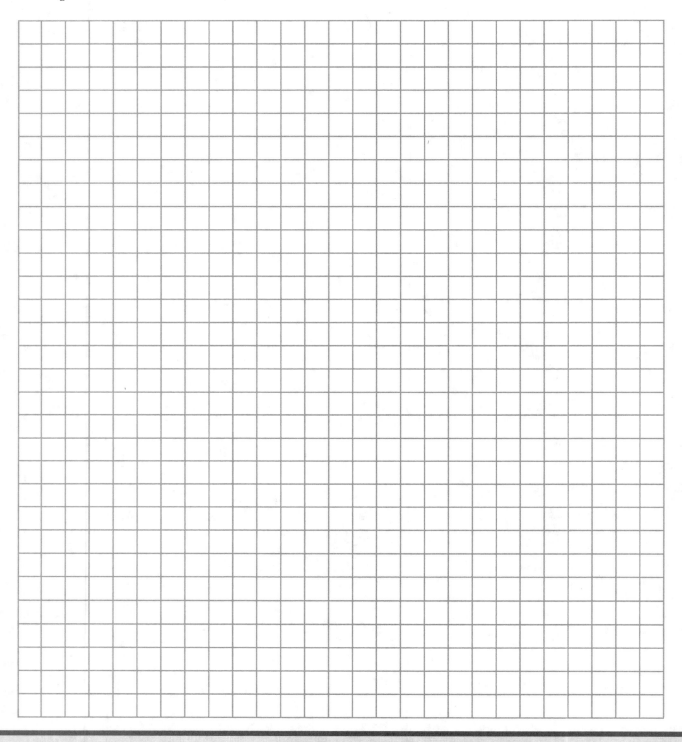

Invented by: _____ Date: _____

Invented by: _____ Date: _____

The above confidential information is witnessed and understood by:

_____ Date: _____

_____ Date: _____

Record of Conception of Invention

Drawing:

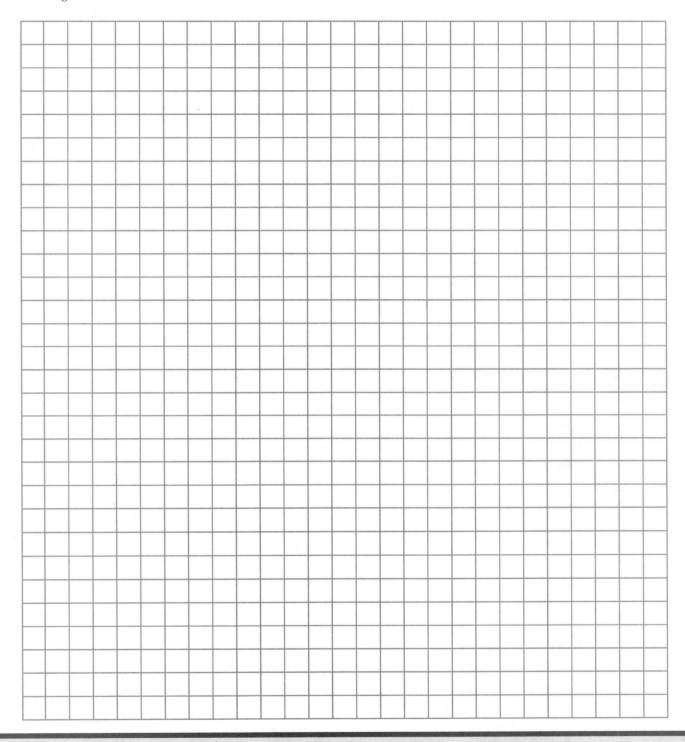

Invented by: _____ Date: _____

Invented by: _____ Date: _____

The above confidential information is witnessed and understood by:

_____ Date: _____

_____ Date: _____

Record of Conception of Invention

Drawing:

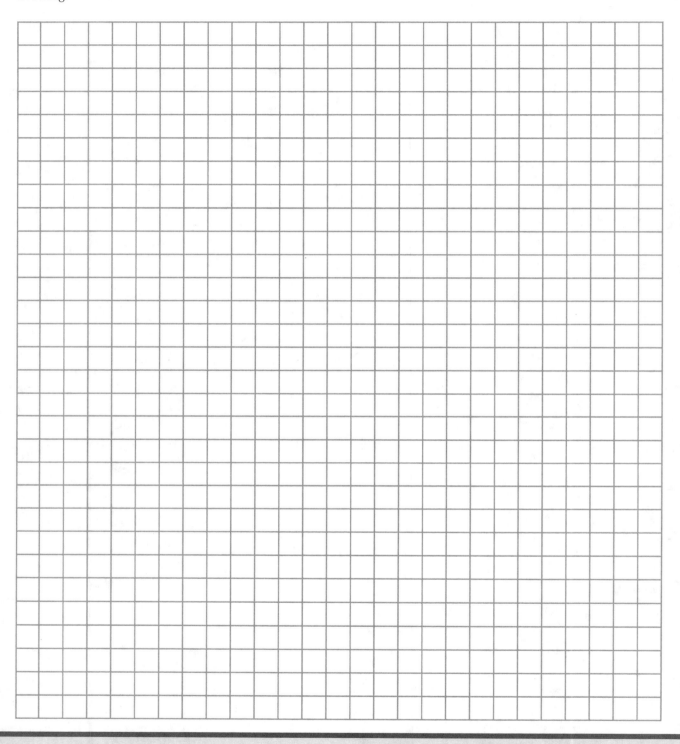

Invented by: _____ Date: _____

Invented by: _____ Date: _____

The above confidential information is witnessed and understood by:

_____ Date: _____

_____ Date: _____

Record of Conception of Invention

Drawing:

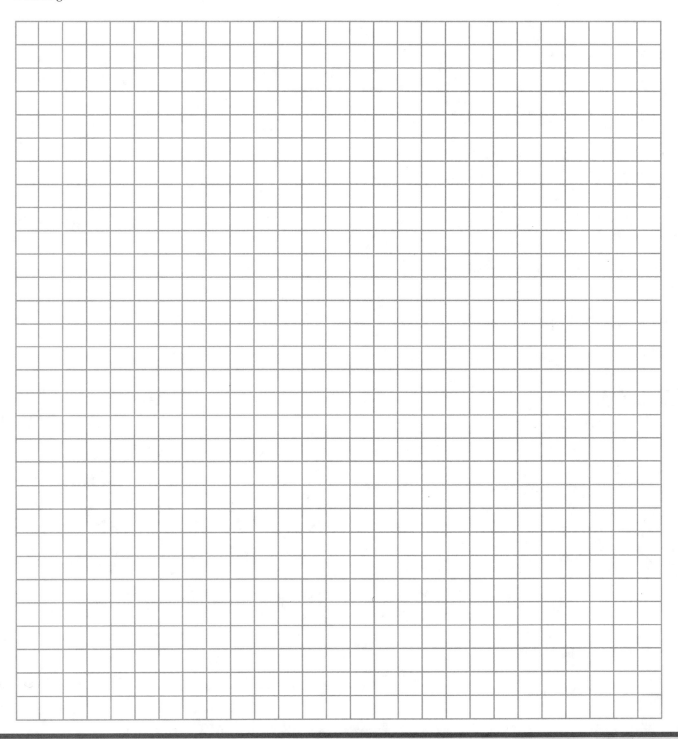

Invented by: _____ Date: _____

Invented by: _____ Date: _____

The above confidential information is witnessed and understood by:

_____ Date: _____

_____ Date: _____

Record of Conception of Invention

Drawing:

Invented by: _____ Date: _____

Invented by: _____ Date: _____

The above confidential information is witnessed and understood by:

_____ Date: _____

_____ Date: _____

Record of Conception of Invention

Drawing:

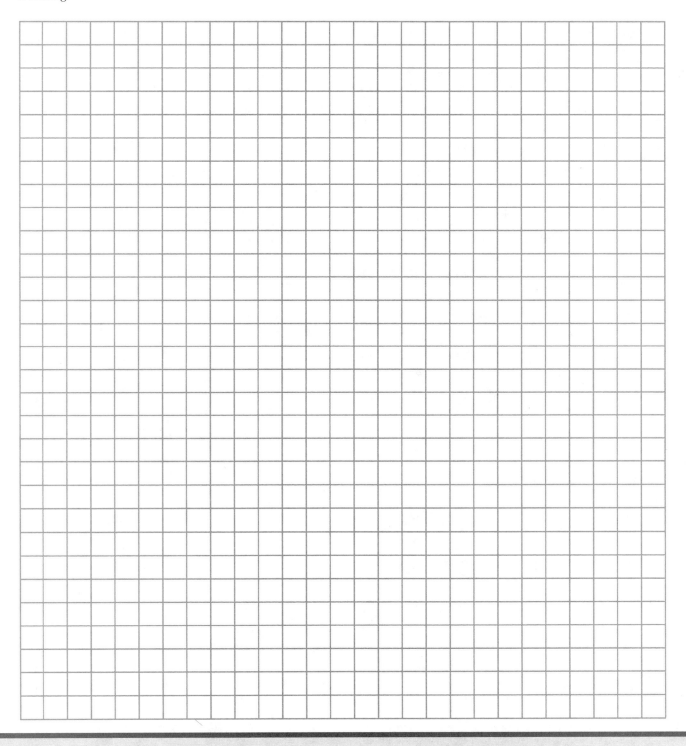

Invented by: _____ Date: _____

Invented by: _____ Date: _____

The above confidential information is witnessed and understood by:

_____ Date: _____

_____ Date: _____

Record of Conception of Invention

Drawing:

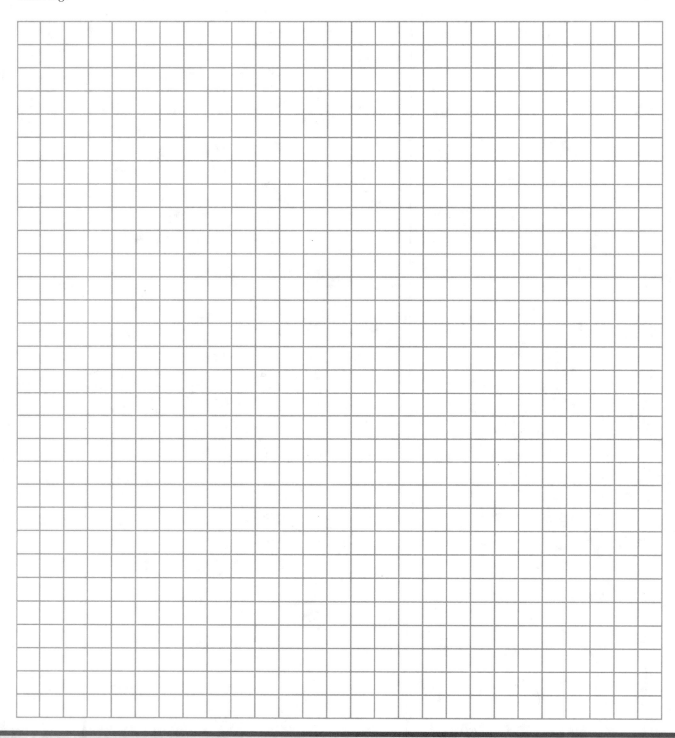

Invented by: _____ Date: _____

Invented by: _____ Date: _____

The above confidential information is witnessed and understood by:

_____ Date: _____

_____ Date: _____

Record of Conception of Invention

Drawing:

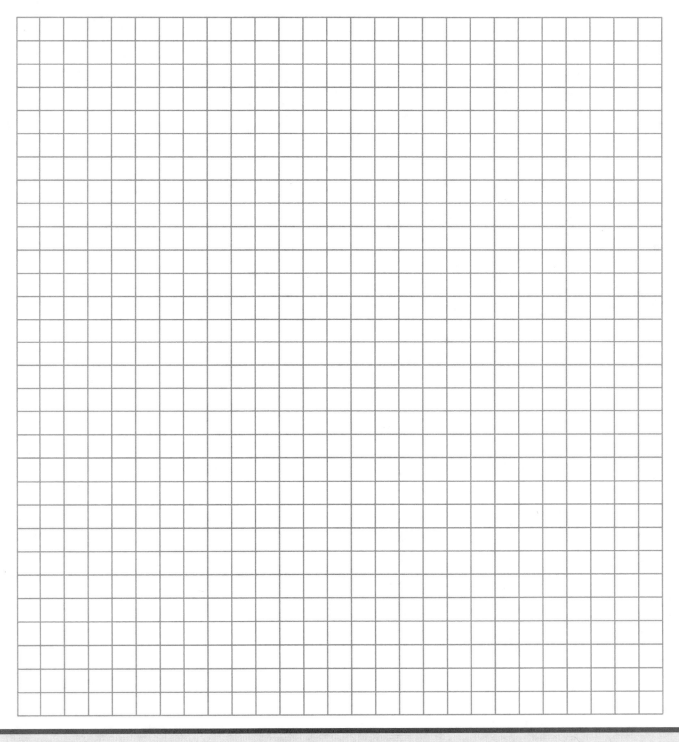

Invented by: _____ Date: _____

Invented by: _____ Date: _____

The above confidential information is witnessed and understood by:

_____ Date: _____

_____ Date: _____

Record of Conception of Invention

Drawing:

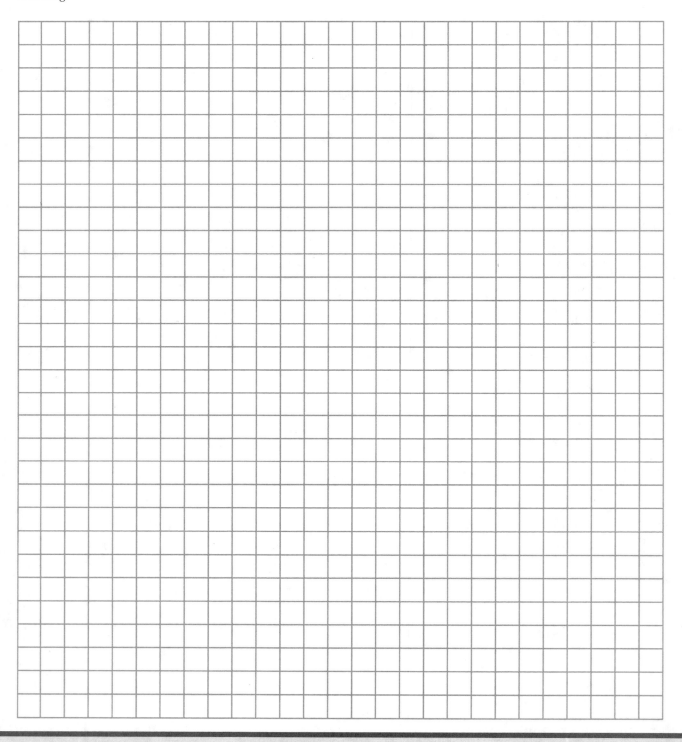

Invented by: _____ Date: _____

Invented by: _____ Date: _____

The above confidential information is witnessed and understood by:

_____ Date: _____

_____ Date: _____

Record of Conception of Invention

Drawing:

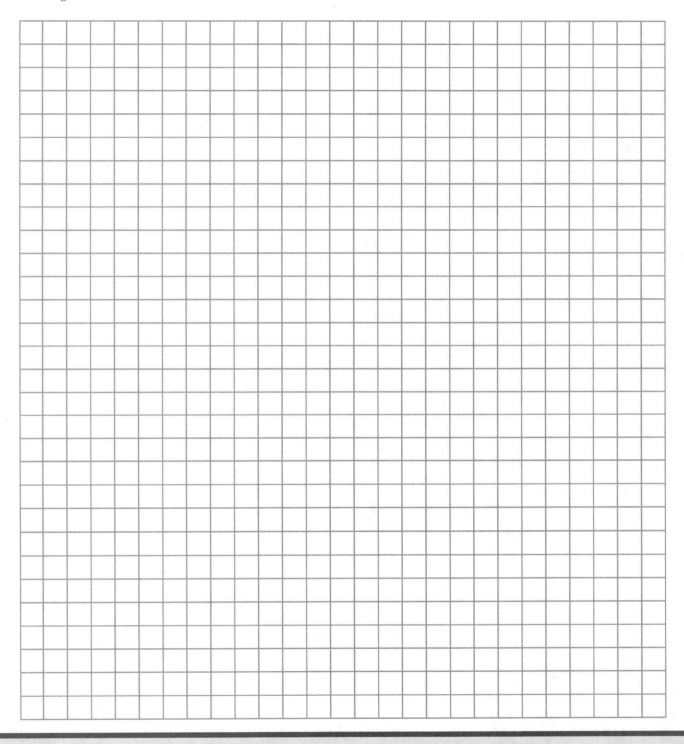

Invented by: _____ Date: _____

Invented by: _____ Date: _____

The above confidential information is witnessed and understood by:

_____ Date: _____

_____ Date: _____

Record of Conception of Invention

Drawing:

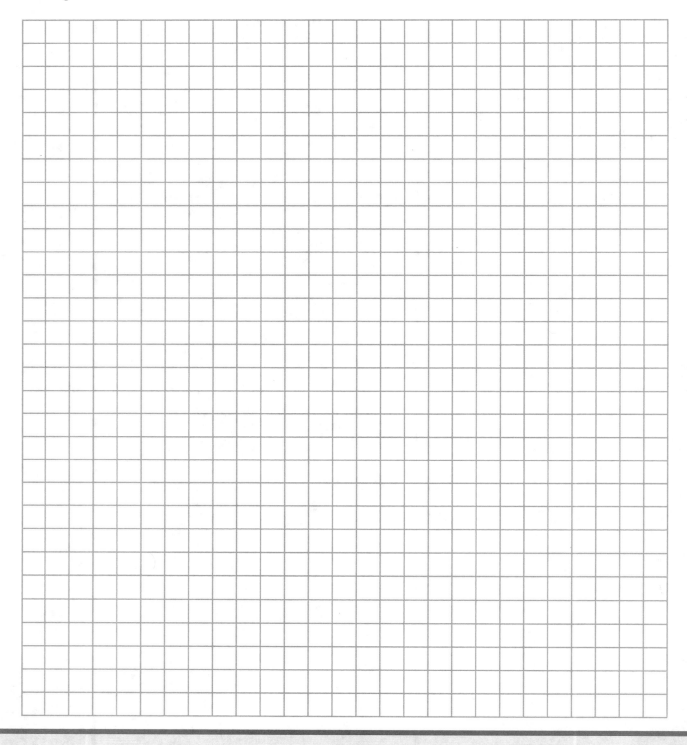

Invented by: _____ Date: _____

Invented by: _____ Date: _____

The above confidential information is witnessed and understood by:

_____ Date: _____

_____ Date: _____

Record of Conception of Invention

Ramifications:

_____

_____

_____

_____

_____

Novel features:

_____

_____

_____

_____

_____

_____

Closest known prior art:

_____

_____

_____

_____

_____

Advantages of my invention:

_____

_____

_____

_____

_____

_____

_____

_____

Invented by: _____ Date: _____

Invented by: _____ Date: _____

The above confidential information is witnessed and understood by:

_____ Date: _____

_____ Date: _____

Record of Conception of Invention

Additional conceptions and ramifications:

_____

_____

_____

_____

_____

_____

_____

_____

_____

_____

_____

_____

_____

_____

_____

_____

_____

_____

_____

_____

_____

_____

_____

_____

_____

_____

_____

_____

_____

_____

_____

_____

_____

Invented by: _____ Date: _____

Invented by: _____ Date: _____

The above confidential information is witnessed and understood by:

_____ Date: _____

_____ Date: _____

Record of Conception of Invention

Additional conceptions and ramifications:

_____

Invented by: _____ Date: _____

Invented by: _____ Date: _____

The above confidential information is witnessed and understood by:

_____ Date: _____

_____ Date: _____

Record of Conception of Invention

Additional conceptions and ramifications:

_____

_____

_____

_____

_____

_____

_____

_____

_____

_____

_____

_____

_____

_____

_____

_____

_____

_____

_____

_____

_____

_____

_____

_____

_____

_____

_____

_____

_____

Invented by: _____ Date: _____

Invented by: _____ Date: _____

The above confidential information is witnessed and understood by:

_____ Date: _____

_____ Date: _____

Record of Building and Testing of Invention

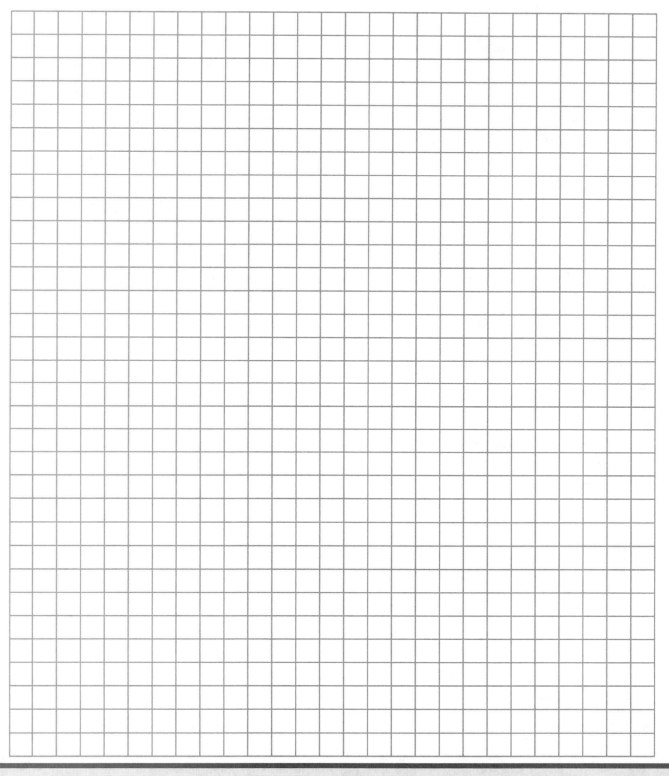

Invented by: _____ Date: _____

Invented by: _____ Date: _____

The above confidential information is witnessed and understood by:

_____ Date: _____

_____ Date: _____

Record of Building and Testing of Invention

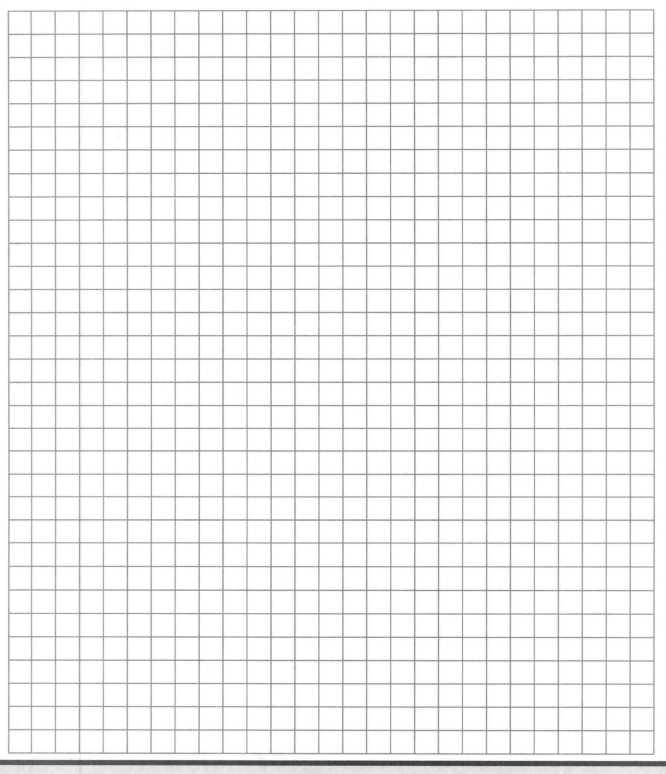

Invented by: _____ Date: _____

Invented by: _____ Date: _____

The above confidential information is witnessed and understood by:

_____ Date: _____

_____ Date: _____

Record of Building and Testing of Invention

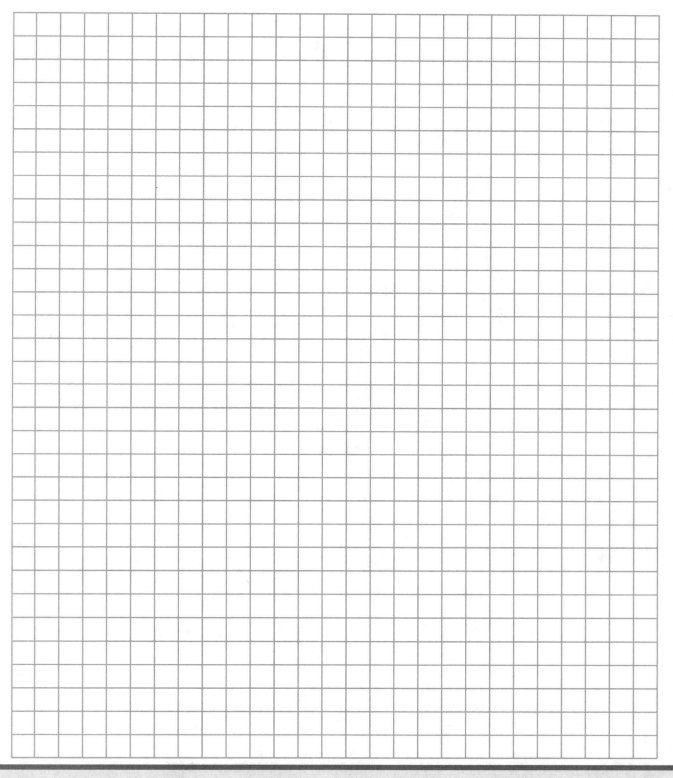

Invented by: _____ Date: _____

Invented by: _____ Date: _____

The above confidential information is witnessed and understood by:

_____ Date: _____

_____ Date: _____

Record of Building and Testing of Invention

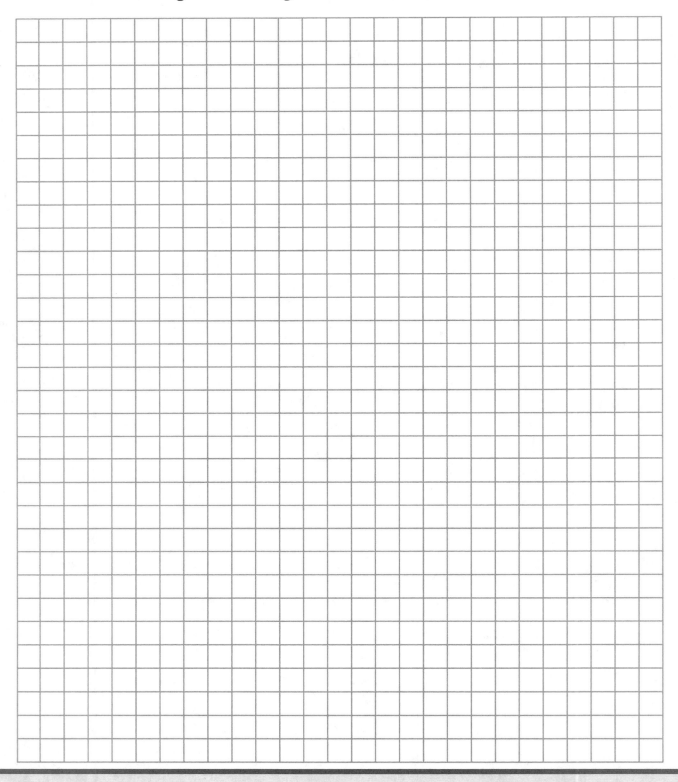

Invented by: _____ Date: _____

Invented by: _____ Date: _____

The above confidential information is witnessed and understood by:

_____ Date: _____

_____ Date: _____

Record of Building and Testing of Invention

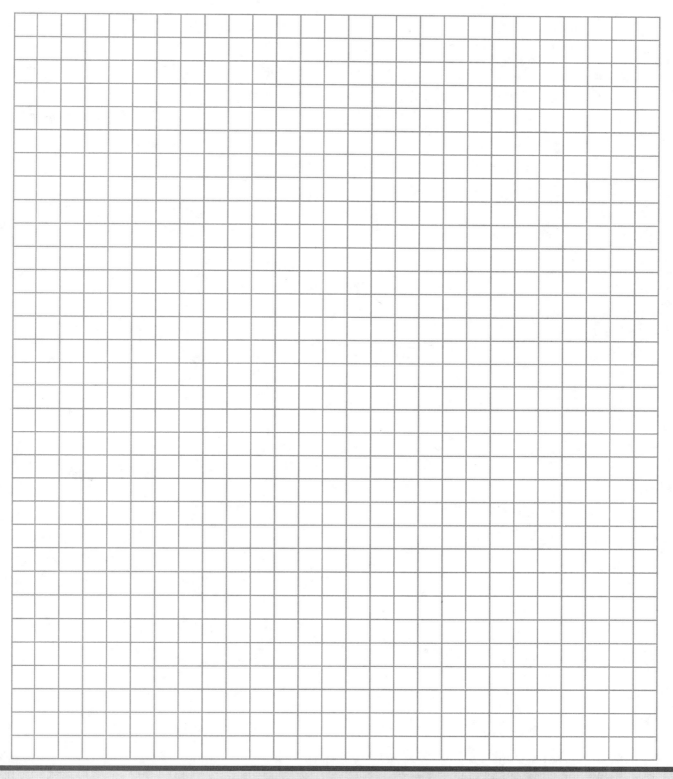

Invented by: _____   Date: _____

Invented by: _____   Date: _____

The above confidential information is witnessed and understood by:

_____   Date: _____

_____   Date: _____

Record of Building and Testing of Invention

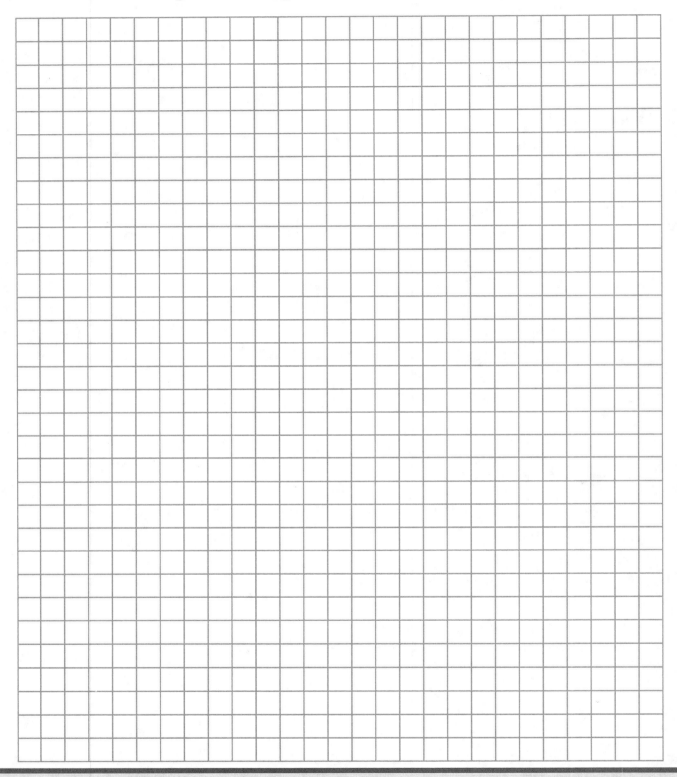

Invented by: _____ Date: _____

Invented by: _____ Date: _____

The above confidential information is witnessed and understood by:

_____ Date: _____

_____ Date: _____

Record of Building and Testing of Invention

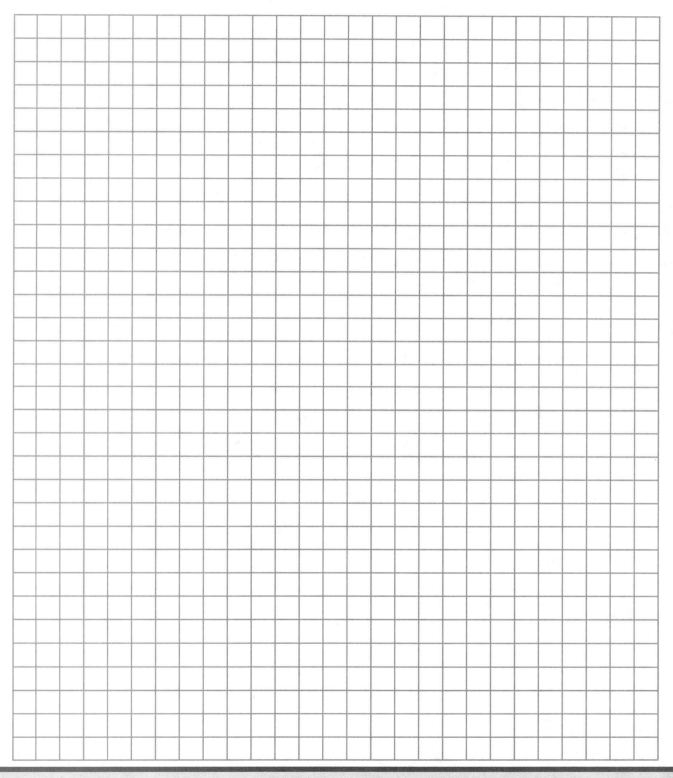

Invented by: _____ Date: _____

Invented by: _____ Date: _____

The above confidential information is witnessed and understood by:

_____ Date: _____

_____ Date: _____

Record of Building and Testing of Invention

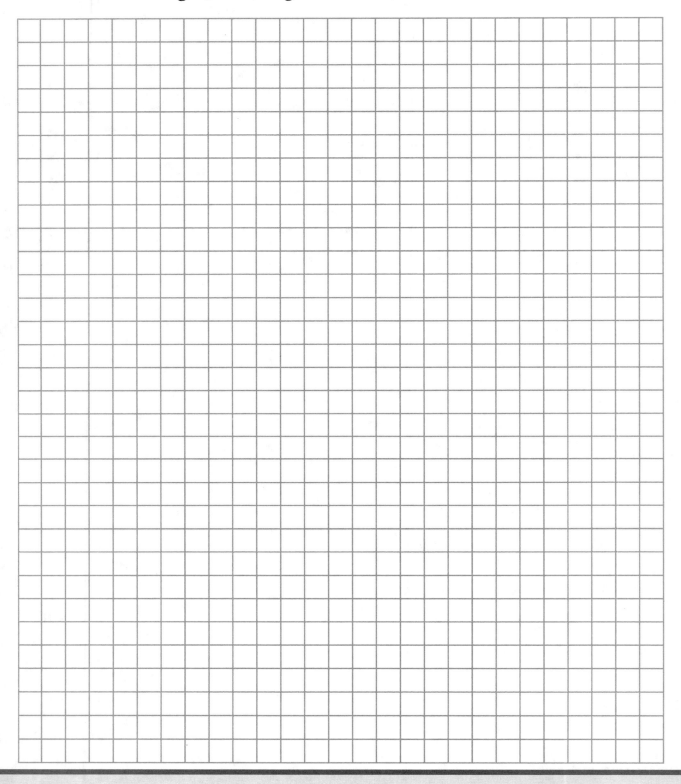

Invented by: _____ Date: _____

Invented by: _____ Date: _____

The above confidential information is witnessed and understood by:

_____ Date: _____

_____ Date: _____

Record of Building and Testing of Invention

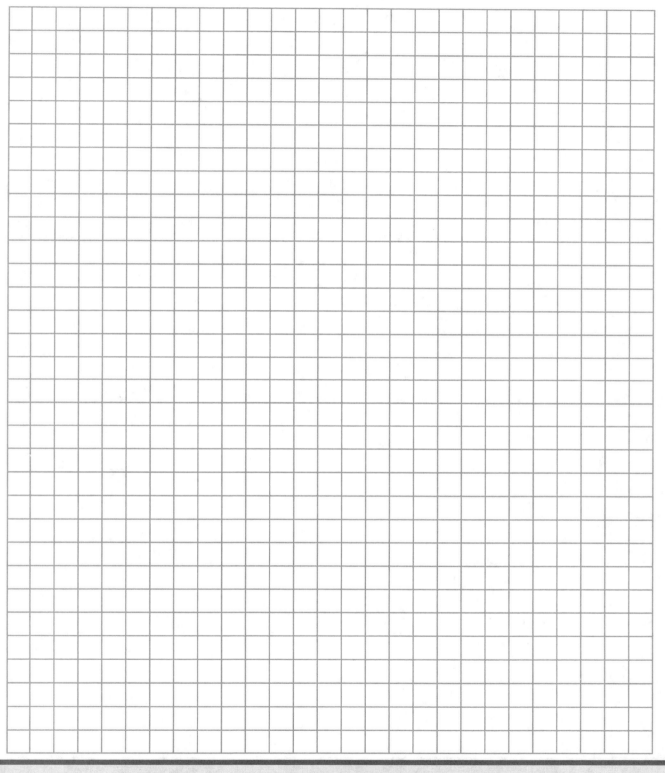

Invented by: _____ Date: _____

Invented by: _____ Date: _____

The above confidential information is witnessed and understood by:

_____ Date: _____

_____ Date: _____

Record of Building and Testing of Invention

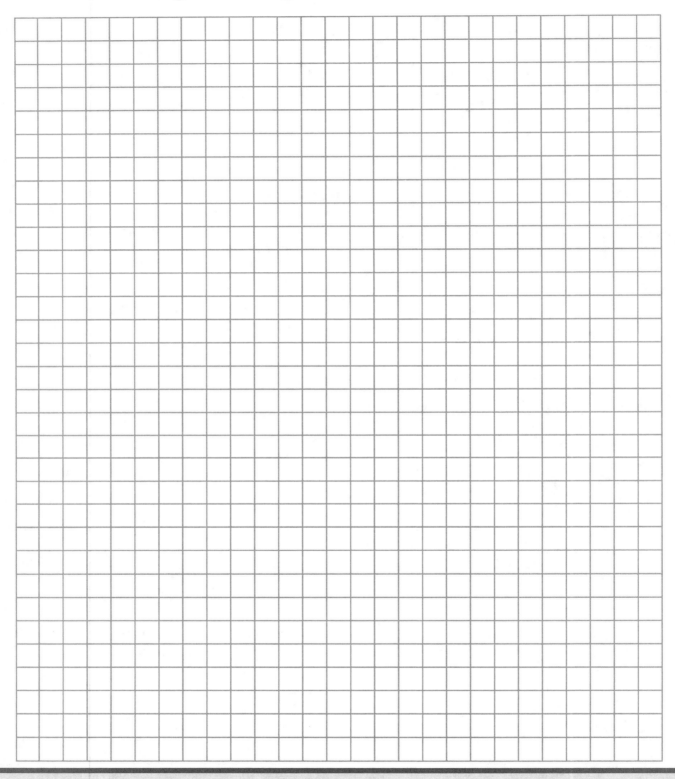

Invented by: _____ Date: _____

Invented by: _____ Date: _____

The above confidential information is witnessed and understood by:

_____ Date: _____

_____ Date: _____

Record of Building and Testing of Invention

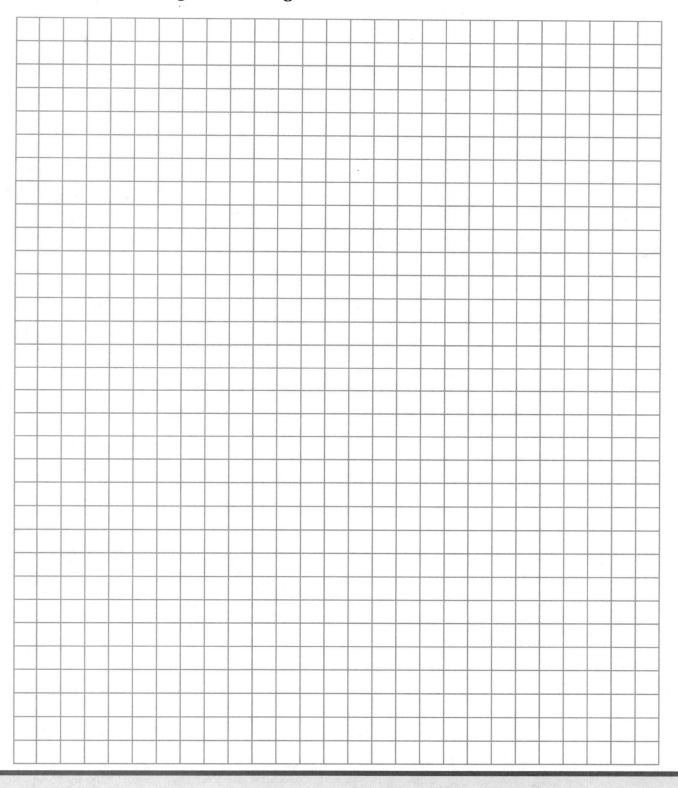

Invented by: _____ Date: _____

Invented by: _____ Date: _____

The above confidential information is witnessed and understood by:

_____ Date: _____

_____ Date: _____

Record of Building and Testing of Invention

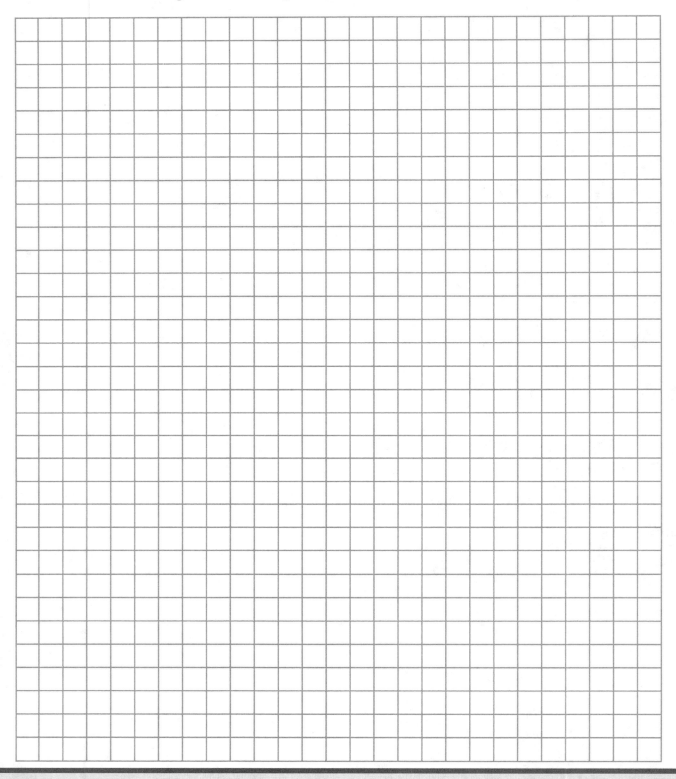

Invented by: _____ Date: _____

Invented by: _____ Date: _____

The above confidential information is witnessed and understood by:

_____ Date: _____

_____ Date: _____

Record of Building and Testing of Invention

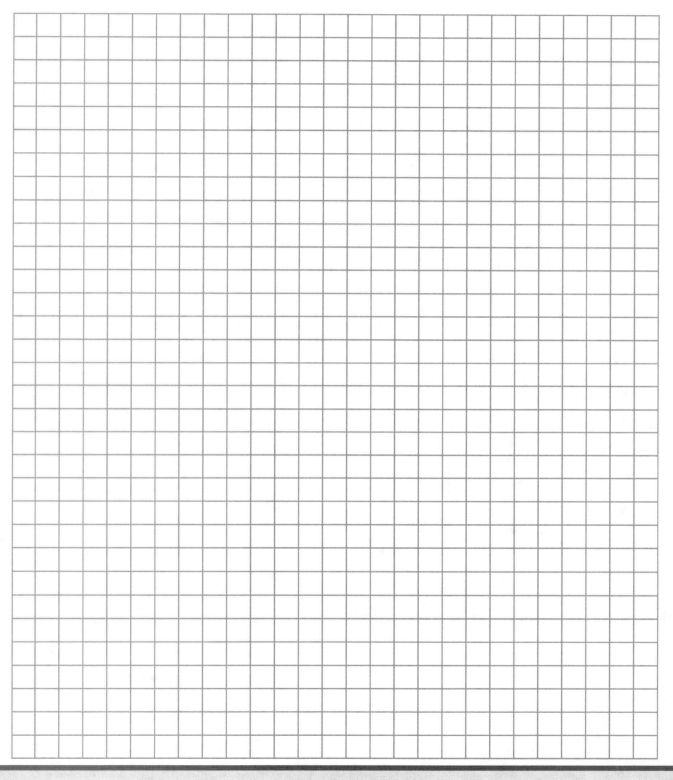

Invented by: _____ Date: _____

Invented by: _____ Date: _____

The above confidential information is witnessed and understood by:

_____ Date: _____

_____ Date: _____

Record of Building and Testing of Invention

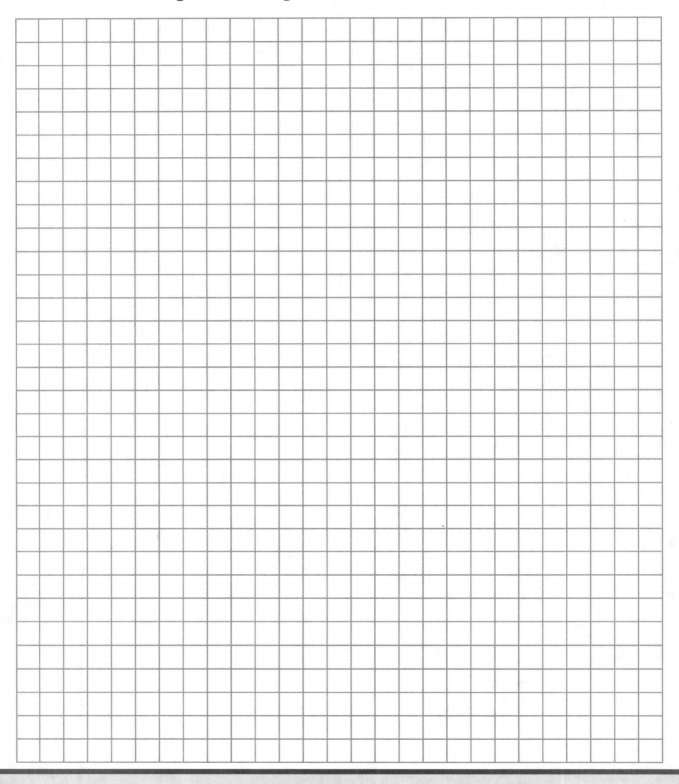

Invented by: _____ Date: _____

Invented by: _____ Date: _____

The above confidential information is witnessed and understood by:

_____ Date: _____

_____ Date: _____

Record of Building and Testing of Invention

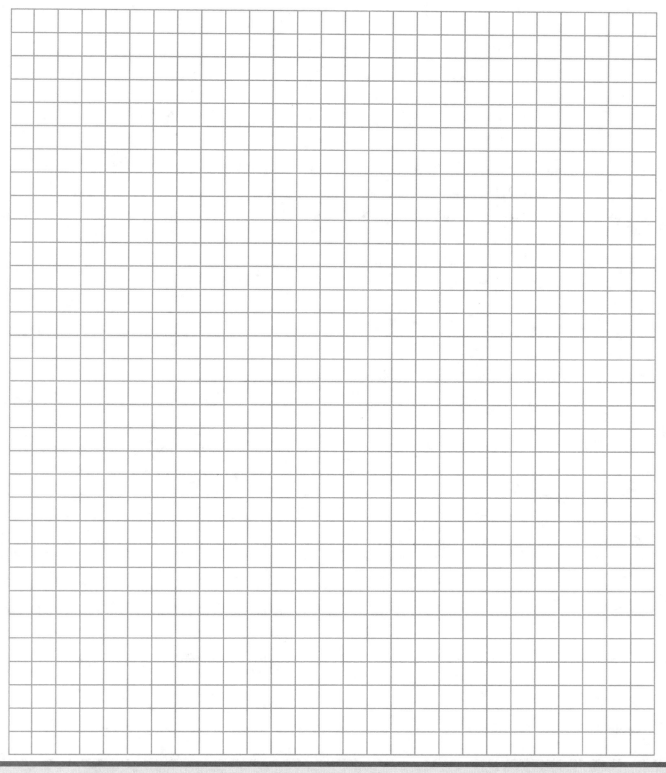

Invented by: _____ Date: _____

Invented by: _____ Date: _____

The above confidential information is witnessed and understood by:

_____ Date: _____

_____ Date: _____

Record of Building and Testing of Invention

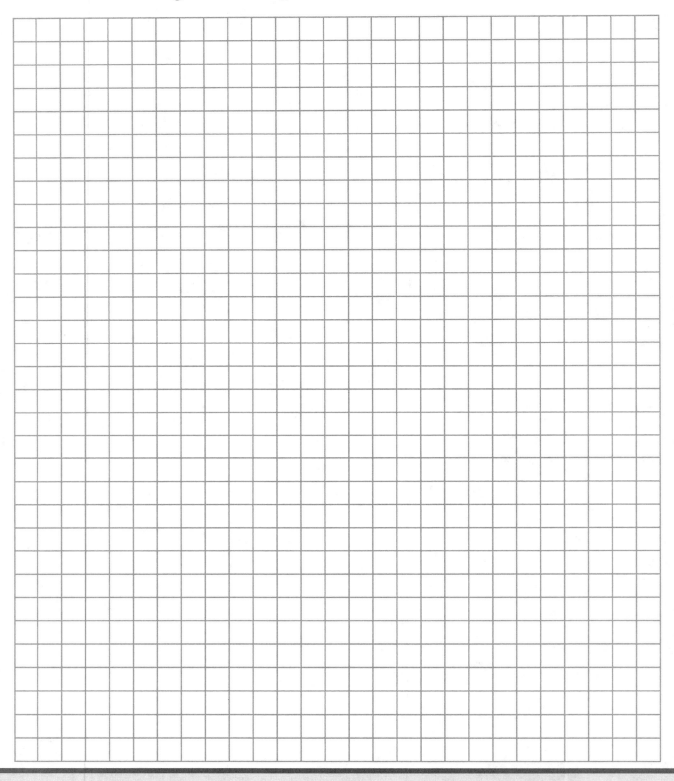

Invented by: _____ Date: _____

Invented by: _____ Date: _____

The above confidential information is witnessed and understood by:

_____ Date: _____

_____ Date: _____

Record of Building and Testing of Invention

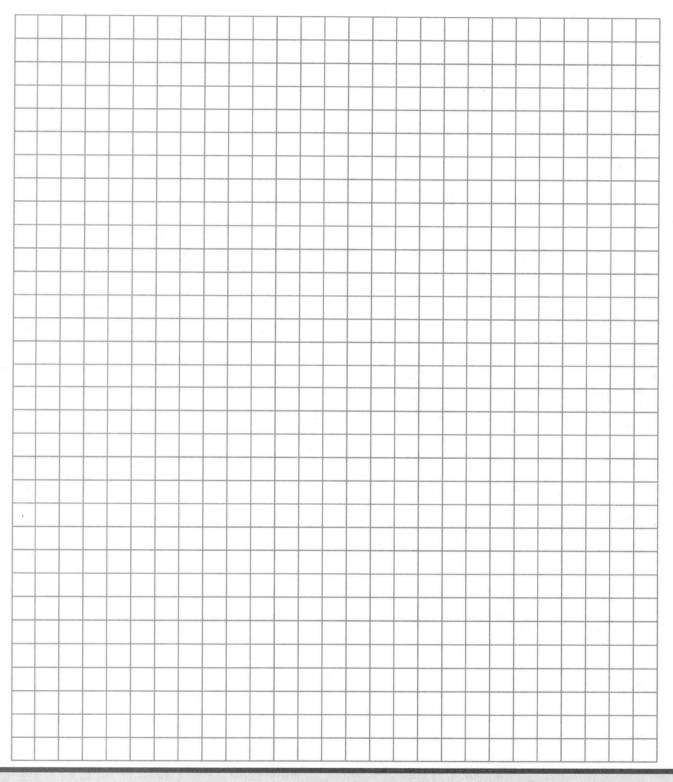

Invented by: _____ Date: _____

Invented by: _____ Date: _____

The above confidential information is witnessed and understood by:

_____ Date: _____

_____ Date: _____

Record of Building and Testing of Invention

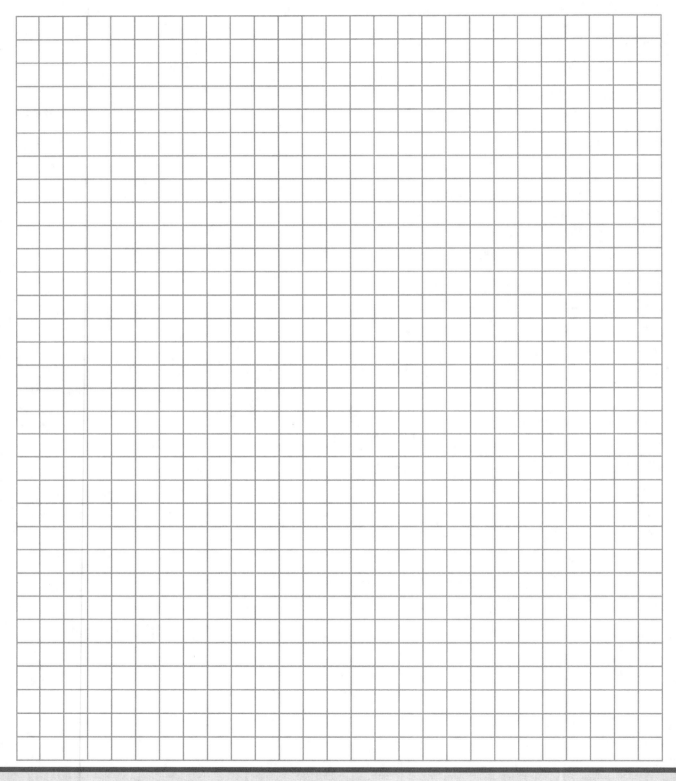

Invented by: _____ Date: _____

Invented by: _____ Date: _____

The above confidential information is witnessed and understood by:

_____ Date: _____

_____ Date: _____

Record of Building and Testing of Invention

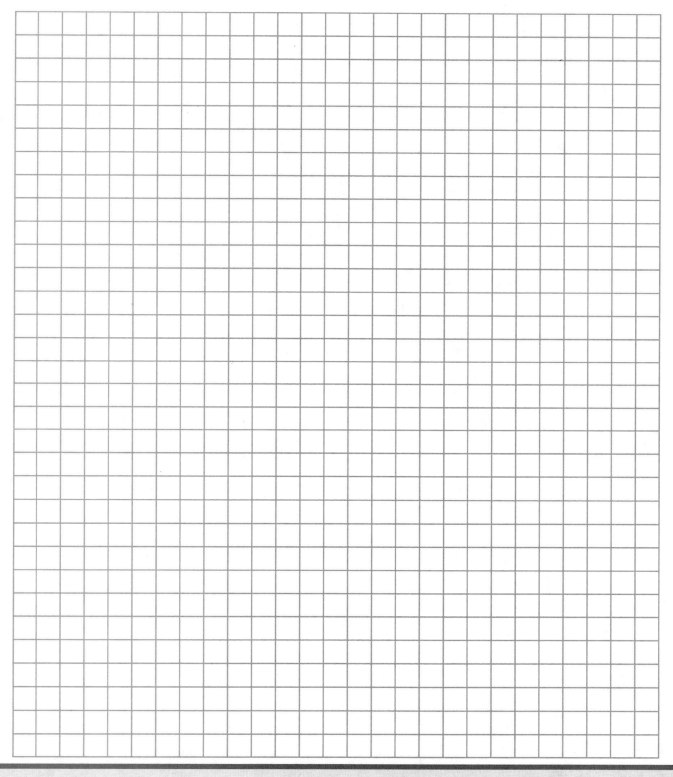

Invented by: _____ Date: _____

Invented by: _____ Date: _____

The above confidential information is witnessed and understood by:

_____ Date: _____

_____ Date: _____

Record of Building and Testing of Invention

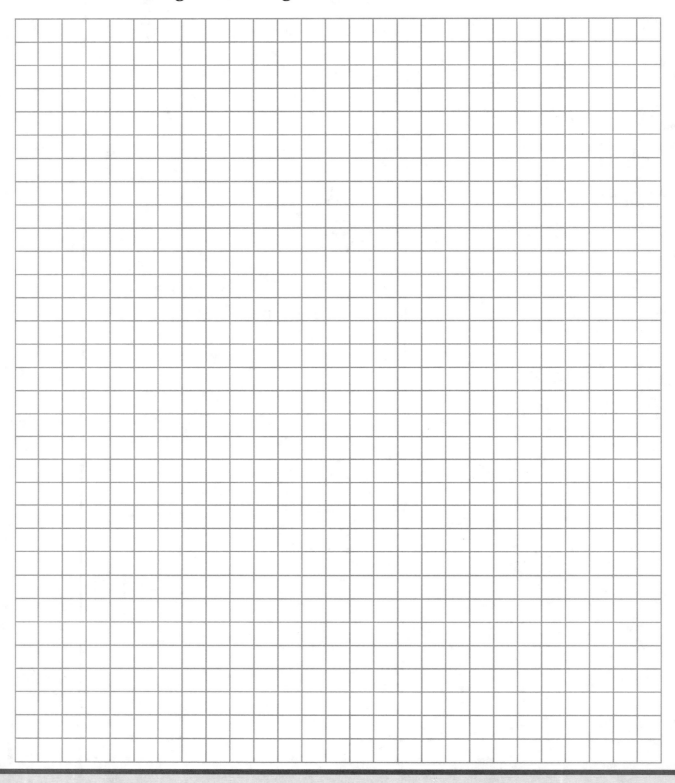

Invented by: _____ Date: _____

Invented by: _____ Date: _____

The above confidential information is witnessed and understood by:

_____ Date: _____

_____ Date: _____

Record of Building and Testing of Invention

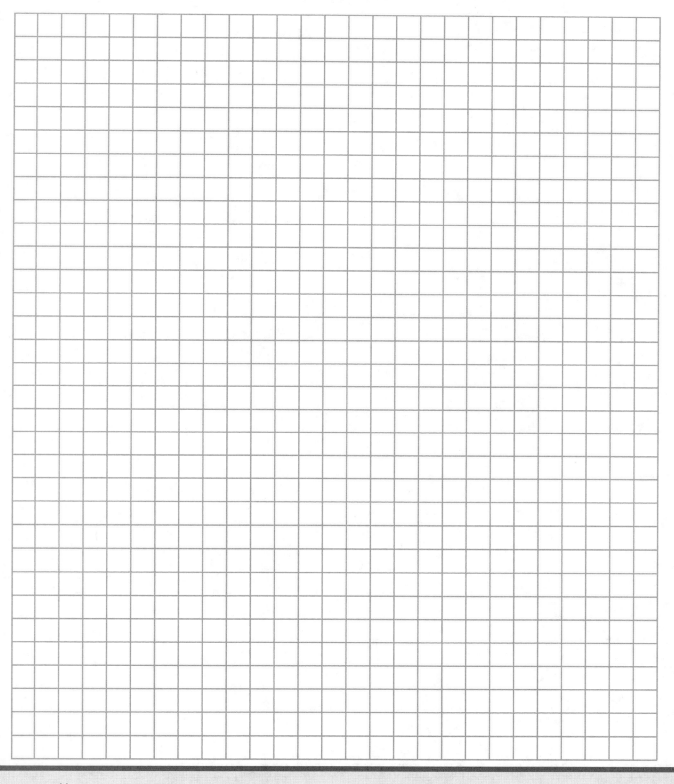

Invented by: _____ Date: _____

Invented by: _____ Date: _____

The above confidential information is witnessed and understood by:

_____ Date: _____

_____ Date: _____

Record of Building and Testing of Invention

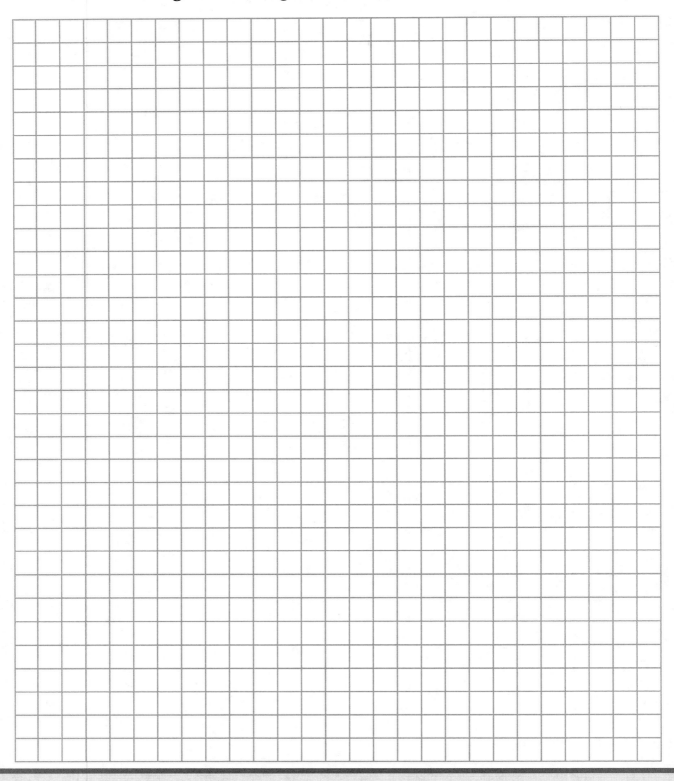

Invented by: _____ Date: _____

Invented by: _____ Date: _____

The above confidential information is witnessed and understood by:

_____ Date: _____

_____ Date: _____

Record of Building and Testing of Invention

Invented by: _____   Date: _____

Invented by: _____   Date: _____

The above confidential information is witnessed and understood by:

_____   Date: _____

_____   Date: _____

Record of Building and Testing of Invention

Invented by: _____   Date: _____

Invented by: _____   Date: _____

The above confidential information is witnessed and understood by:

_____   Date: _____

_____   Date: _____

Other Possible Applications of Invention

1. Alternative application and change required:

_____

_____

_____

_____

_____

2. Alternative application and change required:

_____

_____

_____

_____

_____

3. Alternative application and change required:

_____

_____

_____

_____

_____

4. Alternative application and change required:

_____

_____

_____

_____

_____

5. Alternative application and change required:

_____

_____

_____

_____

_____

Invented by: _____ Date: _____

Invented by: _____ Date: _____

The above confidential information is witnessed and understood by:

_____ Date: _____

_____ Date: _____

Trademark Conception and Protection

Distinctive Name/Design & Goods/Service:

Distinctive Name/Design & Goods/Service:

Invented by: _____ Date: _____

Invented by: _____ Date: _____

The above confidential information is witnessed and understood by:

_____ Date: _____

_____ Date: _____

Trademark Conception and Protection

Distinctive Name/Design & Goods/Service:

Distinctive Name/Design & Goods/Service:

Invented by: _____ Date: _____

Invented by: _____ Date: _____

The above confidential information is witnessed and understood by:

_____ Date: _____

_____ Date: _____

Distinctive Design Conception

Drawing(s)

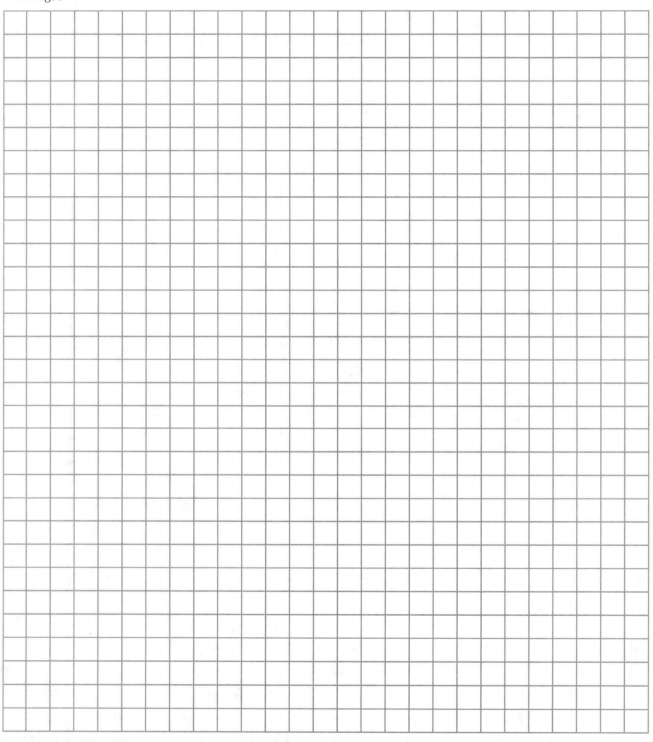

Invented by: _____ Date: _____

Invented by: _____ Date: _____

The above confidential information is witnessed and understood by:

_____ Date: _____

_____ Date: _____

Distinctive Design Conception

Drawing(s)

Invented by: _____ Date: _____

Invented by: _____ Date: _____

The above confidential information is witnessed and understood by:

_____ Date: _____

_____ Date: _____

Distinctive Design Conception

Drawing(s)

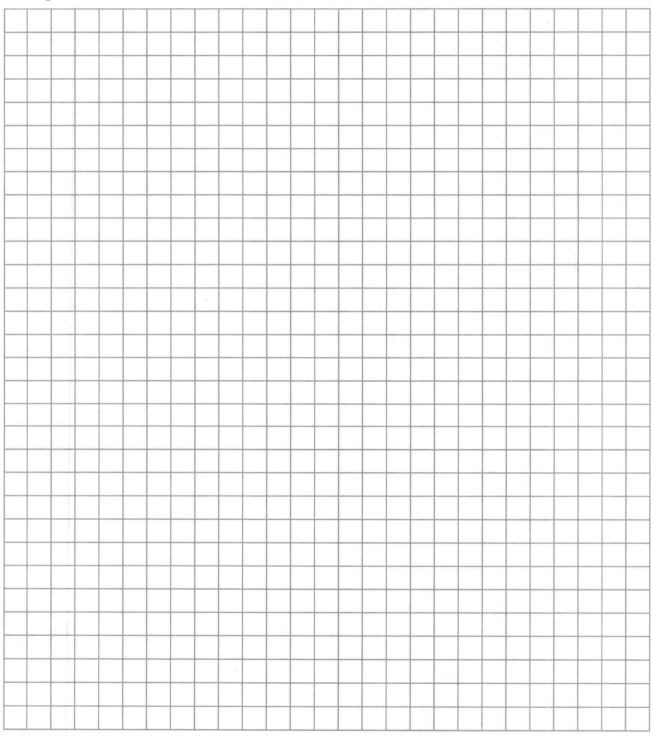

Invented by: _____ Date: _____

Invented by: _____ Date: _____

The above confidential information is witnessed and understood by:

_____ Date: _____

_____ Date: _____

Distinctive Design Conception

Drawing(s)

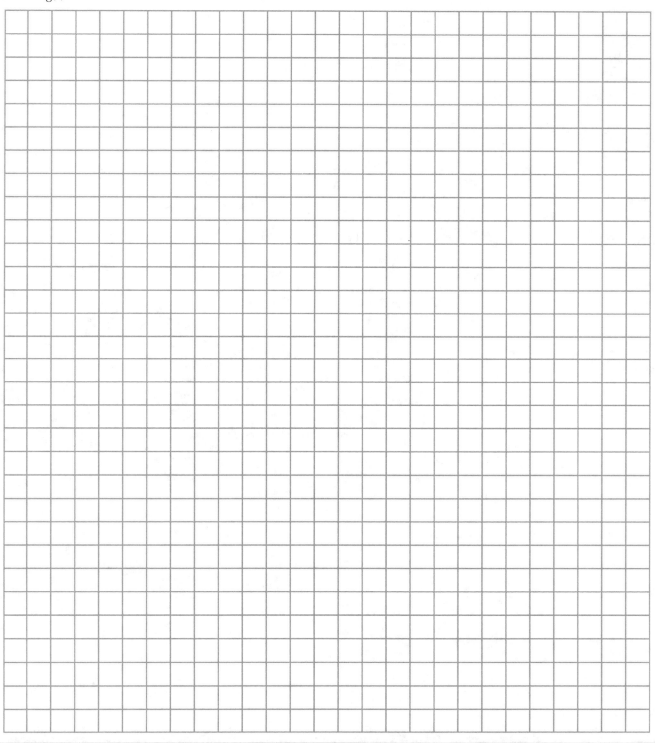

Invented by: _____ Date: _____

Invented by: _____ Date: _____

The above confidential information is witnessed and understood by:

_____ Date: _____

_____ Date: _____

Distinctive Design Conception

Drawing(s)

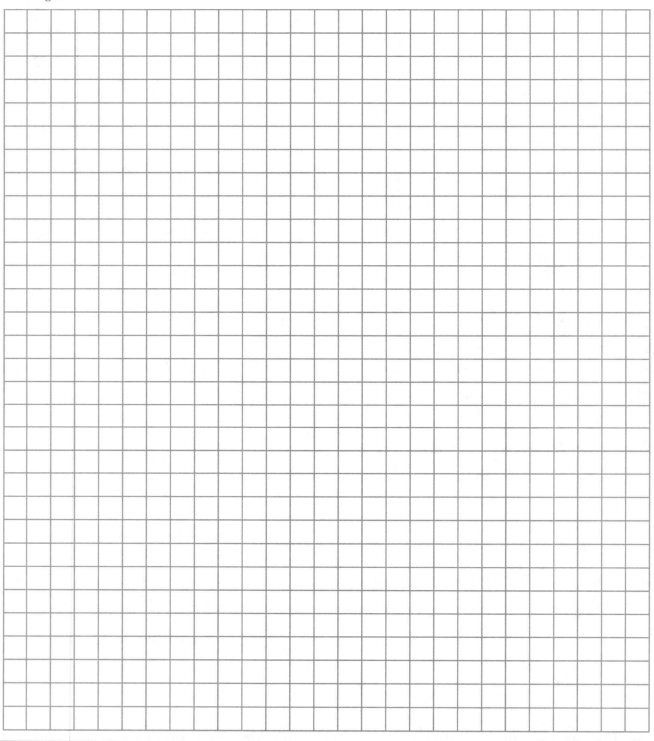

Invented by: _____ Date: _____

Invented by: _____ Date: _____

The above confidential information is witnessed and understood by:

_____ Date: _____

_____ Date: _____

Distinctive Design Conception

Drawing(s)

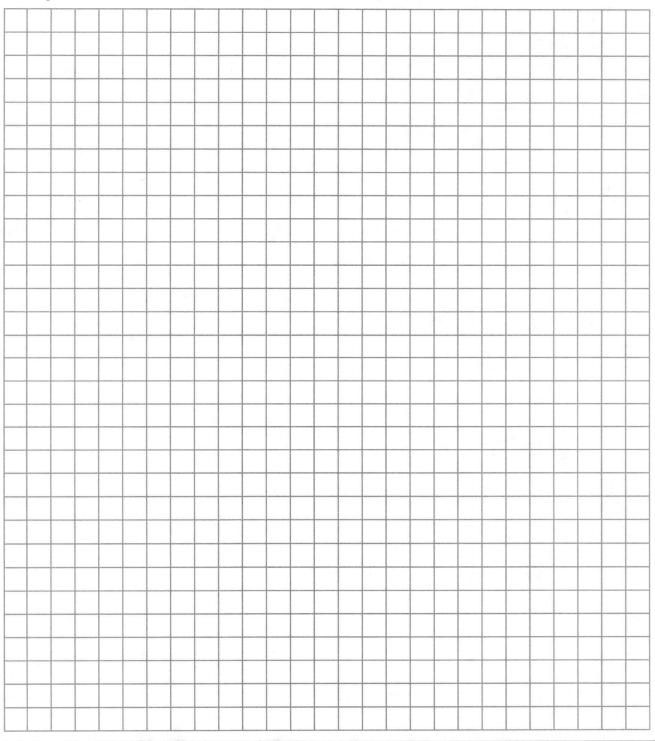

Invented by: _____ Date: _____

Invented by: _____ Date: _____

The above confidential information is witnessed and understood by:

_____ Date: _____

_____ Date: _____

Distinctive Design Conception

Drawing(s)

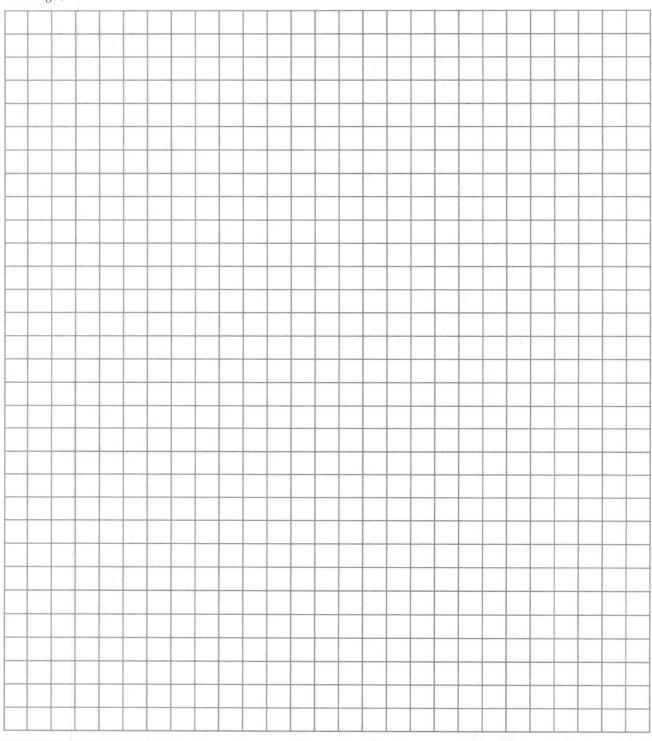

Invented by: _____ Date: _____

Invented by: _____ Date: _____

The above confidential information is witnessed and understood by:

_____ Date: _____

_____ Date: _____

Distinctive Design Conception

Drawing(s)

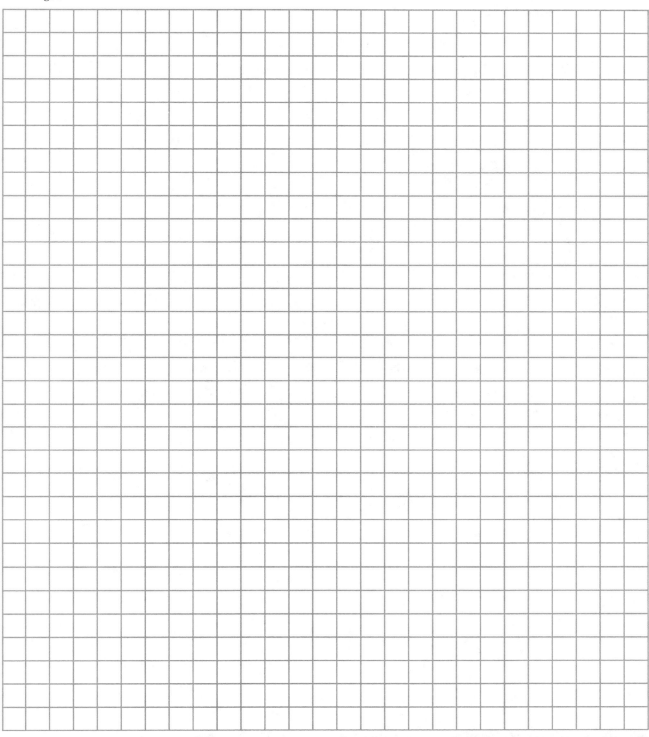

Invented by: _____ Date: _____

Invented by: _____ Date: _____

The above confidential information is witnessed and understood by:

_____ Date: _____

_____ Date: _____

Distinctive Design Conception

Drawing(s)

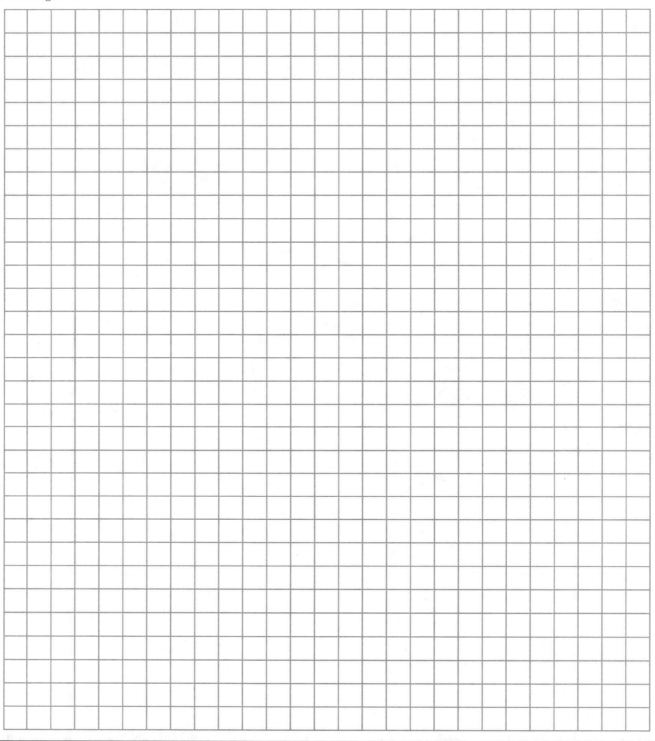

Invented by: _____ Date: _____

Invented by: _____ Date: _____

The above confidential information is witnessed and understood by:

_____ Date: _____

_____ Date: _____

Distinctive Design Conception

Drawing(s)

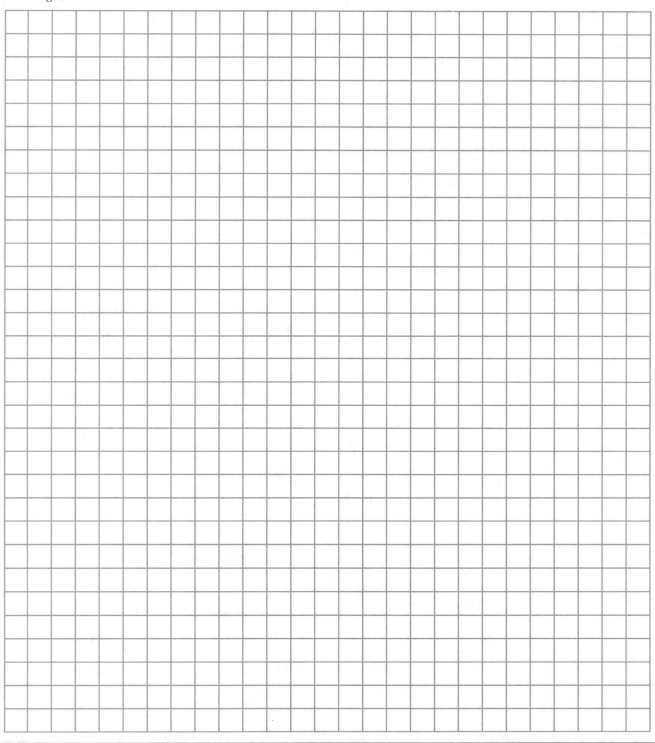

Invented by: _____ Date: _____

Invented by: _____ Date: _____

The above confidential information is witnessed and understood by:

_____ Date: _____

_____ Date: _____

Distinctive Design Conception

Drawing(s)

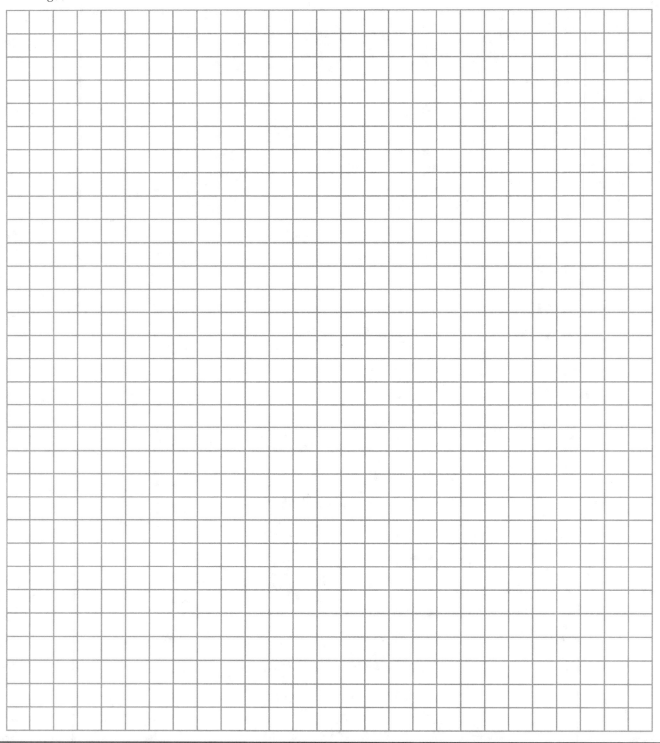

Invented by: _____ Date: _____

Invented by: _____ Date: _____

The above confidential information is witnessed and understood by:

_____ Date: _____

_____ Date: _____

II

Worksheets

Prior Art Search

Steps	Date

1. My earliest provable date of invention:

   _____   _____

   _____   _____

2. Date of the first public use, offer for sale, public disclosure or commercial disclosure of my invention:

   _____   _____

   _____   _____

3. Publications searched:

   a. _____   _____

   b. _____   _____

   c. _____   _____

   d. _____   _____

   e. _____   _____

   f. _____   _____

   g. _____   _____

4. Search of similar products (include stores visited):

   a. _____   _____

   _____

   b. _____   _____

   _____

   c. _____   _____

   _____

   d. _____   _____

   _____

   e. _____   _____

   _____

   f. _____   _____

   _____

   g. _____   _____

   _____

Prior Art Search

Steps	Date

5. Patent search

   Prior relevant U.S. patents discovered (include patent numbers and patent class)

   a. _____   _____

   b. _____   _____

   c. _____   _____

   d. _____   _____

   e. _____   _____

   f. _____   _____

   g. _____   _____

   h. _____   _____

   i. _____   _____

   j. _____   _____

   k. _____   _____

   l. _____   _____

   m. _____   _____

   n. _____

Patentability Checklist

My invention is a new and useful*:

☐ Process or method

☐ Machine (includes electrical circuits)

☐ Article of manufacture

☐ Composition of matter (includes new life forms)

☐ New use of one of the above

These Novel Physical Features**	Produce	These New Unexpected Results

a. _____

_____

_____

_____

_____

b. _____

_____

_____

_____

_____

c. _____

_____

_____

_____

_____

d. _____

_____

_____

_____

_____

a. _____

_____

_____

_____

_____

b. _____

_____

_____

_____

_____

c. _____

_____

_____

_____

_____

d. _____

_____

_____

_____

_____

---

* As long as you can fit your invention into one or more of these categories, it doesn't matter which category you choose. They do overlap to some extent.

** Remember that a novel physical feature can be a novel combination of old physical features.

Patentability Checklist

My invention is a new and useful:

☐ Process or method

☐ Machine (includes electrical circuits)

☐ Article of manufacture

☐ Composition of matter (includes new life forms)

☐ New use of one of the above

These Novel Physical Features	Produce	These New Unexpected Results
a. _____		a. _____
b. _____		b. _____
c. _____		c. _____
d. _____		d. _____

Patentability Checklist

My invention is a new and useful:

☐ Process or method

☐ Machine (includes electrical circuits)

☐ Article of manufacture

☐ Composition of matter (includes new life forms)

☐ New use of one of the above

These Novel Physical Features	Produce	These New Unexpected Results
a. _____		a. _____
_____		_____
_____		_____
_____		_____
_____		_____
_____		_____
b. _____		b. _____
_____		_____
_____		_____
_____		_____
_____		_____
_____		_____
c. _____		c. _____
_____		_____
_____		_____
_____		_____
_____		_____
_____		_____
d. _____		d. _____
_____		_____
_____		_____
_____		_____
_____		_____
_____		_____

Patentability Checklist

My invention is a new and useful:

☐ Process or method

☐ Machine (includes electrical circuits)

☐ Article of manufacture

☐ Composition of matter (includes new life forms)

☐ New use of one of the above

These Novel Physical Features	Produce	These New Unexpected Results
a. _____		a. _____
b. _____		b. _____
c. _____		c. _____
d. _____		d. _____

Document Disclosure Checklist

	Date

☐ 1. Request for Participation in Disclosure Document Program (see Appendix V: Tear-Out Forms)

☐ 2. Check for the specified fee (see Appendix IV: Fee Schedule), payable to the Commissioner for Patents, or if paying by credit card enclose Credit Card Payment Form.

☐ 3. One copy of your Record of Conception of Invention (see Appendix I: Notebook) or Invention Disclosure form (see Appendix V: Tear-Out Forms)

☐ 4. Stamped receipt postcard with your name and address on the front

☐ 5. Envelope addressed to:
Box DD
Commissioner for Patents
Washington, DC 20231

The disclosure sheets (whether notebook entries or completed Invention Disclosure Form) must be numbered. The sheets can be letter size (8$\frac{1}{2}$" x 11") or A4 size (210 mm x 297 mm). You should submit a photocopy of your original signed and witnessed disclosure and keep your original.

Provisional Patent Application Checklist

Date
_____

☐ 1. A description of the invention and its operation, which clearly teaches how to make and use all embodiments of the invention that you might later want to claim. (This should be the equivalent of the information supplied in the Invention Description and Operation Description of the Specification in a regular patent application (RPA).)

☐ 2. Drawing sheets, if necessary to describe invention

☐ 3. Although it's not necessary, we recommend that your PPA include all the parts of a Specification included in an RPA.

☐ 4. Although it's not necessary, we recommend that your PPA contain at least one claim.

☐ 5. A completed Provisional Patent Application Cover including Express Mail section (see Appendix V: Tear-Out Forms)

☐ 6. A check for the specified fee, payable to the Commissioner for Patents (see Appendix IV: Fee Schedule) or, if paying by credit card, enclose Credit Card Payment Form

☐ 7. A stamped receipt postcard with your name and address on the front

☐ 8. Envelope addressed to:
Box DD
Commissioner for Patents
Washington, DC 20231

Patent Application Checklist

	Date

A. Application

    ☐ 1. Return Receipt Postcard addressed to you with all papers listed on back

    ☐ 2. Check or Money Order for correct filing fee (basic fee and fee for any excess claims) or, if paying by credit card, enclose Credit Card Payment Form

    ☐ 3. Transmittal Letter and Fee Transmittal

    ☐ 4. Drawing sheets

    ☐ 5. Specification:

    ☐ 6. Claims

    ☐ 7. Abstract

    ☐ 8. Patent Application Declaration (PAD)

    ☐ 9. Information Disclosure Statement and PTO-1449 with references attached (if you're filing it with your application). Otherwise IDS must be sent within three months.

    ☐ 10. Petition to Make Special (optional to speed application processing)

    ☐ 11. Assignment if needed

    ☐ 12. Disclosure Document Reference Letter if you previously filed a Disclosure Document

    ☐ 13. Envelope addressed to:
        Box Patent Application
        Commissioner for Patents
        Washington, DC 20231

Patent Application Checklist

	Date

B. Amendment _____

- ☐ 1. All pages completed?
- ☐ 2. All points in Office Action answered?
- ☐ 3. If number of claims is increased, is any necessary additional fee enclosed?
- ☐ 4. Certificate of Mailing included?
- ☐ 5. Amendment mailed on time or Petition to Extend with fee included?
- ☐ 6. If Petition to Extend is included, is it properly completed with proper fee?
- ☐ 7. Amendment signed and dated by proper party(ies)?
- ☐ 8. Envelope properly addressed and stamped?
- ☐ 9. Stamped, addressed, properly completed return postcard enclosed?
- ☐ 10. Enough file copies made?

C. Paying Issue Fee _____

- ☐ 1. Issue Fee Transmittal form filled out and signed?
- ☐ 2. If paying by check, is check for correct amount attached and signed?
- ☐ 3. If paying by credit card, is Credit Card Payment Form enclosed?
- ☐ 4. Postcard attached, stamped, addressed?
- ☐ 5. Any needed drawing corrections made?
- ☐ 6. Certificate of Mailing attached, completed, signed, dated?
- ☐ 7. Mailed on time? (Three-month period is not extendable.)
- ☐ 8. Stamped, addressed, properly completed return postcard enclosed?
- ☐ 9. Enough file copies made?

Design Patent Application Checklist

	Date

☐   1. Design Patent Application   _____

☐   2. The Drawing(s)   _____

☐   3. Patent Application Declaration   _____

☐   4. Filing Fee   _____

☐   5. Receipt Postcard   _____

☐   6. Information Disclosure Statement and List of Prior Art Cited   _____

Trademark Use and Registration

Steps	Date

1. Final version of trademark conceived (documented in Section A4)   _____

2. Trademark search completed   _____

   a. Name of searcher

   b. Federally registered trademarks

   c. State registered trademarks

   d. Trade journals and product lists

      i. _____

     ii. _____

    iii. _____

    iv. _____

     v. _____

    vi. _____

   vii. _____

  viii. _____

3. First use of trademark

   a. Intrastate   _____

   b. Interstate   _____

   c. Foreign   _____

Trademark Use and Registration

Steps	Date

4. Registration of trademark with PTO*

   a. Date regular application filed (trademark already in use)   _____

   b. Date application based upon intent to use filed   _____

   c. Date Amendment to Allege Use filed   _____

   d. Date registration granted   _____

   e. Registration # _____   _____

   f. ☐ Principal Register   ☐ Supplemental Register

   g. Class and description of goods:

     _____

     _____

     _____

     _____

5. Renewal of federal registration

   a. §§ 8/15 Declarations due by   _____

   b. Renewal due by   _____

---

* State trademark registration also exists. If you aren't using your invention across states, consider placing it on your state's trademark register.

Record of Contacts

Name & Title	Date	Agreement Signed?

Address & Phone: _____

_____

_____

Comments: _____

_____

_____

Follow up? _____

_____

Name & Title	Date	Agreement Signed?

Address & Phone: _____

_____

_____

Comments: _____

_____

_____

Follow up? _____

_____

Name & Title	Date	Agreement Signed?

Address & Phone: _____

_____

_____

Comments: _____

_____

_____

Follow up? _____

Record of Contacts

Name & Title	Date	Agreement Signed?

Address & Phone: _____

_____

_____

Comments: _____

_____

_____

Follow up? _____

_____

Name & Title	Date	Agreement Signed?

Address & Phone: _____

_____

_____

Comments: _____

_____

_____

Follow up? _____

_____

Name & Title	Date	Agreement Signed?

Address & Phone: _____

_____

_____

Comments: _____

_____

_____

Follow up? _____

Record of Contacts

Name & Title	Date	Agreement Signed?

Address & Phone: _____

_____

_____

Comments: _____

_____

_____

Follow up? _____

_____

Name & Title	Date	Agreement Signed?

Address & Phone: _____

_____

_____

Comments: _____

_____

_____

Follow up? _____

_____

Name & Title	Date	Agreement Signed?

Address & Phone: _____

_____

_____

Comments: _____

_____

_____

Follow up? _____

Record of Contacts

Name & Title	Date	Agreement Signed?

Address & Phone: _____

_____

_____

Comments: _____

_____

_____

Follow up? _____

_____

Name & Title	Date	Agreement Signed?

Address & Phone: _____

_____

_____

Comments: _____

_____

_____

Follow up? _____

_____

Name & Title	Date	Agreement Signed?

Address & Phone: _____

_____

_____

Comments: _____

_____

_____

Follow up? _____

_____

Record of Contacts

Name & Title	Date	Agreement Signed?

Address & Phone: _____

_____

_____

Comments: _____

_____

_____

Follow up? _____

_____

Name & Title	Date	Agreement Signed?

Address & Phone: _____

_____

_____

Comments: _____

_____

_____

Follow up? _____

_____

Name & Title	Date	Agreement Signed?

Address & Phone: _____

_____

_____

Comments: _____

_____

_____

Follow up? _____

_____

Legal Protection Summary

Means of Protection	Date

1. Conception recorded, signed, dated and witnessed

_____
date

2. Disclosure of conception signed, dated, recorded and witnessed

_____
date

3. Disclosure document filed (optional)

_____
date

4. Building and testing recorded, signed, dated, and witnessed

_____
date

5. Provisional Patent Application filed (optional)

_____
date

6. Patent application filed

_____
date

7. Patent pending notice on invention

_____   _____
yes   no

8. Patent application published

_____
date

9. Patent application allowed

_____
date

10. Foreign patent application(s) filed

a. _____

_____
date

b. _____

_____
date

c. _____

_____
date

d. _____

_____
date

e. _____

_____
date

11. Trade secret without patent application

_____   _____
yes   no

12. First trademark use

_____
date

13. State trademark registration

_____
date

14. Trademark registration with PTO

_____
date

15. Design patent application filed

_____
date

16. Design patent approved

_____
date

17. Copyright notice on design, artwork or written materials

_____   _____
yes   no

18. Copyright registered

_____
date

19. Sold invention before filing for patent

_____
date

Positive and Negative Factors Evaluation

Inventor(s): _____

_____

Invention: _____

_____

Factor	Weight (−100 to +100)
1. Cost	_____
2. Weight	_____
3. Size	_____
4. Safety/Health	_____
5. Speed	_____
6. Ease of Use	_____
7. Ease of Production	_____
8. Durability	_____
9. Repairability	_____
10. Novelty	_____
11. Convenience/Social Benefit	_____
12. Reliability	_____
13. Ecology	_____
14. Salability	_____
15. Appearance	_____
16. Viewability	_____
17. Precision	_____
18. Noise	_____
19. Odor	_____
20. Taste	_____
21. Market Size	_____
22. Trend of Demand	_____
23. Seasonal Demand	_____
24. Difficulty of Market Penetration	_____
25. Potential Competition	_____
26. Quality	_____
27. Excitement	_____

Factor	Weight (−100 to +100)
28. Markup	_____
29. Inferior Performance	_____
30. "Sexy" Packaging	_____
31. Miscellaneous	_____
32. Long Life Cycle	_____
33. Related Product Addability	_____
34. Satisfies Existing Need	_____
35. Legality	_____
36. Operability	_____
37. Development	_____
38. Profitability	_____
39. Obsolescence	_____
40. Incompatibility	_____
41. Product Liability Risk	_____
42. Market Dependence	_____
43. Difficulty of Distribution	_____
44. Service Requirements	_____
45. New Tooling Required	_____
46. Inertia Must Be Overcome	_____
47. Too Advanced Technically	_____
48. Substantial Learning Required	_____
49. Difficult to Promote	_____
50. Lack of Market	_____
51. Crowded Field	_____
52. Commodities	_____
53. Combination Products	_____
54. Entrenched Competition	_____
55. Instant Anachronism	_____

Total Positive _____

Less: Total Negative _____

NET: _____

Signed: _____ Date: _____

Positive and Negative Factors Evaluation

Inventor(s): _____   Invention: _____

_____   _____

Factor	Weight (–100 to +100)	Factor	Weight (–100 to +100)
1. Cost	_____	28. Markup	_____
2. Weight	_____	29. Inferior Performance	_____
3. Size	_____	30. "Sexy" Packaging	_____
4. Safety/Health	_____	31. Miscellaneous	_____
5. Speed	_____	32. Long Life Cycle	_____
6. Ease of Use	_____	33. Related Product Addability	_____
7. Ease of Production	_____	34. Satisfies Existing Need	_____
8. Durability	_____	35. Legality	_____
9. Repairability	_____	36. Operability	_____
10. Novelty	_____	37. Development	_____
11. Convenience/Social Benefit	_____	38. Profitability	_____
12. Reliability	_____	39. Obsolescence	_____
13. Ecology	_____	40. Incompatibility	_____
14. Salability	_____	41. Product Liability Risk	_____
15. Appearance	_____	42. Market Dependence	_____
16. Viewability	_____	43. Difficulty of Distribution	_____
17. Precision	_____	44. Service Requirements	_____
18. Noise	_____	45. New Tooling Required	_____
19. Odor	_____	46. Inertia Must Be Overcome	_____
20. Taste	_____	47. Too Advanced Technically	_____
21. Market Size	_____	48. Substantial Learning Required	_____
22. Trend of Demand	_____	49. Difficult to Promote	_____
23. Seasonal Demand	_____	50. Lack of Market	_____
24. Difficulty of Market Penetration	_____	51. Crowded Field	_____
25. Potential Competition	_____	52. Commodities	_____
26. Quality	_____	53. Combination Products	_____
27. Excitement	_____	54. Entrenched Competition	_____
		55. Instant Anachronism	_____

Total Positive _____

Less: Total Negative _____

NET: _____

Signed: _____   Date: _____

Positive and Negative Factors Evaluation

Inventor(s): _____

_____

Invention: _____

Factor	Weight (−100 to +100)
1. Cost	_____
2. Weight	_____
3. Size	_____
4. Safety/Health	_____
5. Speed	_____
6. Ease of Use	_____
7. Ease of Production	_____
8. Durability	_____
9. Repairability	_____
10. Novelty	_____
11. Convenience/Social Benefit	_____
12. Reliability	_____
13. Ecology	_____
14. Salability	_____
15. Appearance	_____
16. Viewability	_____
17. Precision	_____
18. Noise	_____
19. Odor	_____
20. Taste	_____
21. Market Size	_____
22. Trend of Demand	_____
23. Seasonal Demand	_____
24. Difficulty of Market Penetration	_____
25. Potential Competition	_____
26. Quality	_____
27. Excitement	_____

Factor	Weight (−100 to +100)
28. Markup	_____
29. Inferior Performance	_____
30. "Sexy" Packaging	_____
31. Miscellaneous	_____
32. Long Life Cycle	_____
33. Related Product Addability	_____
34. Satisfies Existing Need	_____
35. Legality	_____
36. Operability	_____
37. Development	_____
38. Profitability	_____
39. Obsolescence	_____
40. Incompatibility	_____
41. Product Liability Risk	_____
42. Market Dependence	_____
43. Difficulty of Distribution	_____
44. Service Requirements	_____
45. New Tooling Required	_____
46. Inertia Must Be Overcome	_____
47. Too Advanced Technically	_____
48. Substantial Learning Required	_____
49. Difficult to Promote	_____
50. Lack of Market	_____
51. Crowded Field	_____
52. Commodities	_____
53. Combination Products	_____
54. Entrenched Competition	_____
55. Instant Anachronism	_____

Total Positive _____

Less: Total Negative _____

NET: _____

Signed: _____ Date: _____

Positive and Negative Factors Evaluation

Inventor(s): _____   Invention: _____

_____   _____

Factor	Weight (–100 to +100)	Factor	Weight (–100 to +100)
1. Cost	_____	28. Markup	_____
2. Weight	_____	29. Inferior Performance	_____
3. Size	_____	30. "Sexy" Packaging	_____
4. Safety/Health	_____	31. Miscellaneous	_____
5. Speed	_____	32. Long Life Cycle	_____
6. Ease of Use	_____	33. Related Product Addability	_____
7. Ease of Production	_____	34. Satisfies Existing Need	_____
8. Durability	_____	35. Legality	_____
9. Repairability	_____	36. Operability	_____
10. Novelty	_____	37. Development	_____
11. Convenience/Social Benefit	_____	38. Profitability	_____
12. Reliability	_____	39. Obsolescence	_____
13. Ecology	_____	40. Incompatibility	_____
14. Salability	_____	41. Product Liability Risk	_____
15. Appearance	_____	42. Market Dependence	_____
16. Viewability	_____	43. Difficulty of Distribution	_____
17. Precision	_____	44. Service Requirements	_____
18. Noise	_____	45. New Tooling Required	_____
19. Odor	_____	46. Inertia Must Be Overcome	_____
20. Taste	_____	47. Too Advanced Technically	_____
21. Market Size	_____	48. Substantial Learning Required	_____
22. Trend of Demand	_____	49. Difficult to Promote	_____
23. Seasonal Demand	_____	50. Lack of Market	_____
24. Difficulty of Market Penetration	_____	51. Crowded Field	_____
25. Potential Competition	_____	52. Commodities	_____
26. Quality	_____	53. Combination Products	_____
27. Excitement	_____	54. Entrenched Competition	_____
		55. Instant Anachronism	_____

Total Positive _____

Less: Total Negative _____

NET: _____

Signed: _____   Date: _____

Positive and Negative Factors Evaluation

Inventor(s): _____

Invention: _____

Factor	Weight (−100 to +100)	Factor	Weight (−100 to +100)
1. Cost	_____	28. Markup	_____
2. Weight	_____	29. Inferior Performance	_____
3. Size	_____	30. "Sexy" Packaging	_____
4. Safety/Health	_____	31. Miscellaneous	_____
5. Speed	_____	32. Long Life Cycle	_____
6. Ease of Use	_____	33. Related Product Addability	_____
7. Ease of Production	_____	34. Satisfies Existing Need	_____
8. Durability	_____	35. Legality	_____
9. Repairability	_____	36. Operability	_____
10. Novelty	_____	37. Development	_____
11. Convenience/Social Benefit	_____	38. Profitability	_____
12. Reliability	_____	39. Obsolescence	_____
13. Ecology	_____	40. Incompatibility	_____
14. Salability	_____	41. Product Liability Risk	_____
15. Appearance	_____	42. Market Dependence	_____
16. Viewability	_____	43. Difficulty of Distribution	_____
17. Precision	_____	44. Service Requirements	_____
18. Noise	_____	45. New Tooling Required	_____
19. Odor	_____	46. Inertia Must Be Overcome	_____
20. Taste	_____	47. Too Advanced Technically	_____
21. Market Size	_____	48. Substantial Learning Required	_____
22. Trend of Demand	_____	49. Difficult to Promote	_____
23. Seasonal Demand	_____	50. Lack of Market	_____
24. Difficulty of Market Penetration	_____	51. Crowded Field	_____
25. Potential Competition	_____	52. Commodities	_____
26. Quality	_____	53. Combination Products	_____
27. Excitement	_____	54. Entrenched Competition	_____
		55. Instant Anachronism	_____

Total Positive _____

Less: Total Negative _____

NET: _____

Signed: _____   Date: _____

Potential User Survey

Name and Date		**Agreement Signed?**

1. _____ ☐ Yes   ☐ No

Comments: _____

_____

_____

_____

_____

_____

_____

_____

_____

_____

_____

Signed: _____ Date: _____

Name and Date		**Agreement Signed?**

2. _____ ☐ Yes   ☐ No

Comments: _____

_____

_____

_____

_____

_____

_____

_____

_____

_____

_____

Signed: _____ Date: _____

Potential User Survey

Name and Date	Agreement Signed?

3. _____   ☐ Yes   ☐ No

Comments: _____

_____

_____

_____

_____

_____

_____

_____

_____

_____

_____

_____

_____

Signed: _____   Date: _____

Name and Date	Agreement Signed?

4. _____   ☐ Yes   ☐ No

Comments: _____

_____

_____

_____

_____

_____

_____

_____

_____

_____

_____

Signed: _____   Date: _____

Potential User Survey

Name and Date	Agreement Signed?

5. _____ ☐ Yes ☐ No

Comments: _____

_____

_____

_____

_____

_____

_____

_____

_____

_____

_____

Signed: _____ Date: _____

Name and Date	Agreement Signed?

6. _____ ☐ Yes ☐ No

Comments: _____

_____

_____

_____

_____

_____

_____

_____

_____

_____

Signed: _____ Date: _____

Potential User Survey

Name and Date	Agreement Signed?

7. _____ ☐ Yes ☐ No

Comments: _____

_____

_____

_____

_____

_____

_____

_____

_____

_____

_____

_____

Signed: _____ Date: _____

Name and Date	Agreement Signed?

8. _____ ☐ Yes ☐ No

Comments: _____

_____

_____

_____

_____

_____

_____

_____

_____

_____

_____

_____

Signed: _____ Date: _____

Potential User Survey

Name and Date	Agreement Signed?

9. _____ ☐ Yes   ☐ No

Comments: _____

_____

_____

_____

_____

_____

_____

_____

_____

_____

_____

Signed: _____ Date: _____

Name and Date	Agreement Signed?

10. _____ ☐ Yes   ☐ No

Comments: _____

_____

_____

_____

_____

_____

_____

_____

_____

_____

_____

Signed: _____ Date: _____

Regional Buying Patterns of Related Products

	Product Name	Source of Information	Sales for Last Year Surveyed	Projected Sales
Region: _____				
Product A				
Product B				
Product C				
Product D				
Product E				
Region: _____				
Product A				
Product B				
Product C				
Product D				
Product E				
Region: _____				
Product A				
Product B				
Product C				
Product D				
Product E				
Region: _____				
Product A				
Product B				
Product C				
Product D				
Product E				

Regional Buying Patterns of Related Products

	Product Name	Source of Information	Sales for Last Year Surveyed	Projected Sales
Region:				
Product A				
Product B				
Product C				
Product D				
Product E				
Region:				
Product A				
Product B				
Product C				
Product D				
Product E				
Region:				
Product A				
Product B				
Product C				
Product D				
Product E				
Region:				
Product A				
Product B				
Product C				
Product D				
Product E				

Regional Buying Patterns of Related Products

	Product Name	Source of Information	Sales for Last Year Surveyed	Projected Sales
Region:	_____			
Product A	_____	_____	_____	_____
Product B	_____	_____	_____	_____
Product C	_____	_____	_____	_____
Product D	_____	_____	_____	_____
Product E	_____	_____	_____	_____
Region:	_____			
Product A	_____	_____	_____	_____
Product B	_____	_____	_____	_____
Product C	_____	_____	_____	_____
Product D	_____	_____	_____	_____
Product E	_____	_____	_____	_____
Region:	_____			
Product A	_____	_____	_____	_____
Product B	_____	_____	_____	_____
Product C	_____	_____	_____	_____
Product D	_____	_____	_____	_____
Product E	_____	_____	_____	_____
Region:	_____			
Product A	_____	_____	_____	_____
Product B	_____	_____	_____	_____
Product C	_____	_____	_____	_____
Product D	_____	_____	_____	_____
Product E	_____	_____	_____	_____

Predictions for Targeted Buying Groups

	Potential Purchasers	Age	Sex	Other	Predicted % of Sales
Group 1	_____	_____	_____	_____	_____
Group 2	_____	_____	_____	_____	_____
Group 3	_____	_____	_____	_____	_____
	Source of Information			**Last Year Surveyed**	**Projected**

GROUP 1

% of Population

Region 1	_____	_____	_____
Region 2	_____	_____	_____
Region 3	_____	_____	_____

Disposable Income

Region 1	_____	_____	_____
Region 2	_____	_____	_____
Region 3	_____	_____	_____

GROUP 2

% of Population

Region 1	_____	_____	_____
Region 2	_____	_____	_____
Region 3	_____	_____	_____

Disposable Income

Region 1	_____	_____	_____
Region 2	_____	_____	_____
Region 3	_____	_____	_____

GROUP 3

% of Population

Region 1	_____	_____	_____
Region 2	_____	_____	_____
Region 3	_____	_____	_____

Disposable Income

Region 1	_____	_____	_____
Region 2	_____	_____	_____
Region 3	_____	_____	_____

Predictions for Targeted Buying Groups

	Potential Purchasers	Age	Sex	Other	Predicted % of Sales
Group 1					
Group 2					
Group 3					

Source of Information	Last Year Surveyed	Projected

GROUP 1

% of Population

Region 1 _____   _____   _____

Region 2 _____   _____   _____

Region 3 _____   _____   _____

Disposable Income

Region 1 _____   _____   _____

Region 2 _____   _____   _____

Region 3 _____   _____   _____

GROUP 2

% of Population

Region 1 _____   _____   _____

Region 2 _____   _____   _____

Region 3 _____   _____   _____

Disposable Income

Region 1 _____   _____   _____

Region 2 _____   _____   _____

Region 3 _____   _____   _____

GROUP 3

% of Population

Region 1 _____   _____   _____

Region 2 _____   _____   _____

Region 3 _____   _____   _____

Disposable Income

Region 1 _____   _____   _____

Region 2 _____   _____   _____

Region 3 _____   _____   _____

Predictions for Targeted Buying Groups

	Potential Purchasers	Age	Sex	Other	Predicted % of Sales
Group 1	_____	____	____	_____	_____
Group 2	_____	____	____	_____	_____
Group 3	_____	____	____	_____	_____
	Source of Information			**Last Year Surveyed**	**Projected**

GROUP 1

% of Population

Region 1 _____ _____ _____

Region 2 _____ _____ _____

Region 3 _____ _____ _____

Disposable Income

Region 1 _____ _____ _____

Region 2 _____ _____ _____

Region 3 _____ _____ _____

GROUP 2

% of Population

Region 1 _____ _____ _____

Region 2 _____ _____ _____

Region 3 _____ _____ _____

Disposable Income

Region 1 _____ _____ _____

Region 2 _____ _____ _____

Region 3 _____ _____ _____

GROUP 3

% of Population

Region 1 _____ _____ _____

Region 2 _____ _____ _____

Region 3 _____ _____ _____

Disposable Income

Region 1 _____ _____ _____

Region 2 _____ _____ _____

Region 3 _____ _____ _____

Conclusions Regarding Marketing Trends

The demand for my product will likely increase because of these factors:

_____

_____

_____

_____

_____

_____

_____

_____

_____

The demand could decrease because of these factors:

_____

_____

_____

_____

_____

_____

_____

_____

_____

To take advantage of the positive trends and overcome any projected negative developments, I propose to market my product in the following ways:

_____

_____

_____

_____

_____

_____

_____

_____

_____

_____

_____

Conclusions Regarding Marketing Trends

The demand for my product will likely increase because of these factors:

_____

_____

_____

_____

_____

_____

_____

_____

The demand could decrease because of these factors:

_____

_____

_____

_____

_____

_____

_____

_____

To take advantage of the positive trends and overcome any projected negative developments, I propose to market my product in the following ways:

_____

_____

_____

_____

_____

_____

_____

_____

_____

_____

_____

Conclusions Regarding Marketing Trends

The demand for my product will likely increase because of these factors:

_____

_____

_____

_____

_____

_____

_____

_____

The demand could decrease because of these factors:

_____

_____

_____

_____

_____

_____

_____

_____

To take advantage of the positive trends and overcome any projected negative developments, I propose to market my product in the following ways:

_____

_____

_____

_____

_____

_____

_____

_____

_____

_____

_____

Manufacturer/Distributor Evaluation

If I Want to Distribute Myself

1. Items needed

    a. Facilities:_____

    _____

    b. Inventory:_____

    _____

    c. Employees:_____

    _____

    d. New skills:_____

    _____

    e. Advertising:_____

    _____

2. Funds needed: _____

    _____

3. Distribution options: _____

    _____

4. Sales volume desired: _____

    _____

5. Time needed to achieve sales volume: _____

    _____

6. Liability risks: _____

    _____

7. Time needed to recover costs: _____

    _____

8. Percent per unit that would be paid to an existing distributor: _____

    _____

Conclusions: _____

_____

_____

_____

_____

_____

Manufacturer/Distributor Evaluation

If I Want to Distribute Myself

1. Items needed

    a. Facilities: _____

    _____

    b. Inventory: _____

    _____

    c. Employees: _____

    _____

    d. New skills: _____

    _____

    e. Advertising: _____

    _____

2. Funds needed: _____

    _____

3. Distribution options: _____

    _____

4. Sales volume desired: _____

    _____

5. Time needed to achieve sales volume: _____

    _____

6. Liability risks: _____

    _____

7. Time needed to recover costs: _____

    _____

8. Percent per unit that would be paid to an existing distributor: _____

    _____

Conclusions: _____

_____

_____

_____

_____

_____

_____

Choosing the Right Company

Choice Number _____

a. Name and Location: _____

_____

_____

_____

b. Officers: _____

_____

_____

_____

c. Current Products: _____

_____

_____

d. Sales Volume: _____

_____

e. Advertising Budget: _____

_____

f. Other: _____

_____

Choice Number _____

a. Name and Location: _____

_____

_____

_____

b. Officers: _____

_____

_____

_____

c. Current Products: _____

_____

_____

d. Sales Volume: _____

_____

e. Advertising Budget: _____

_____

f. Other: _____

_____

Choosing the Right Company

Choice Number _____

a. Name and Location: _____

_____

_____

_____

b. Officers: _____

_____

_____

_____

c. Current Products: _____

_____

_____

d. Sales Volume: _____

_____

e. Advertising Budget: _____

_____

f. Other: _____

_____

Choice Number _____

a. Name and Location: _____

_____

_____

_____

b. Officers: _____

_____

_____

_____

c. Current Products: _____

_____

_____

d. Sales Volume: _____

_____

e. Advertising Budget: _____

_____

f. Other: _____

_____

Choosing the Right Company

Choice Number _____

a. Name and Location: _____

_____

_____

_____

b. Officers: _____

_____

_____

_____

c. Current Products: _____

_____

_____

d. Sales Volume: _____

_____

e. Advertising Budget: _____

_____

f. Other: _____

_____

Choice Number _____

a. Name and Location: _____

_____

_____

_____

b. Officers: _____

_____

_____

_____

c. Current Products: _____

_____

_____

d. Sales Volume: _____

_____

e. Advertising Budget: _____

_____

f. Other: _____

_____

Budget

Purpose	High Estimate	Middle Estimate	Low Estimate
1. Build working model			
Parts	_____	_____	_____
Labor	_____	_____	_____
Subtotal	_____	_____	_____
2. Testing			
Parts	_____	_____	_____
Labor	_____	_____	_____
Subtotal	_____	_____	_____
3. Obtain Legal Protection			
Labor	_____	_____	_____
Legal fees	_____	_____	_____
Subtotal	_____	_____	_____
4. Test Marketing			
Survey	_____	_____	_____
Number of units	_____	_____	_____
Advertising/publicity	_____	_____	_____
Subtotal	_____	_____	_____
5. Establish Production			
Facilities	_____	_____	_____
Materials	_____	_____	_____
Employees	_____	_____	_____
Subtotal	_____	_____	_____
6. Other	_____	_____	_____
7. Grand Total	_____	_____	_____

Budget

Purpose	High Estimate	Middle Estimate	Low Estimate
1. Build working model			
Parts	_____	_____	_____
Labor	_____	_____	_____
Subtotal	_____	_____	_____
2. Testing			
Parts	_____	_____	_____
Labor	_____	_____	_____
Subtotal	_____	_____	_____
3. Obtain Legal Protection			
Labor	_____	_____	_____
Legal fees	_____	_____	_____
Subtotal	_____	_____	_____
4. Test Marketing			
Survey	_____	_____	_____
Number of units	_____	_____	_____
Advertising/publicity	_____	_____	_____
Subtotal	_____	_____	_____
5. Establish Production			
Facilities	_____	_____	_____
Materials	_____	_____	_____
Employees	_____	_____	_____
Subtotal	_____	_____	_____
6. Other	_____	_____	_____
7. Grand Total	_____	_____	_____

Budget

Purpose	High Estimate	Middle Estimate	Low Estimate
1. Build working model			
Parts	_____	_____	_____
Labor	_____	_____	_____
Subtotal	_____	_____	_____
2. Testing			
Parts	_____	_____	_____
Labor	_____	_____	_____
Subtotal	_____	_____	_____
3. Obtain Legal Protection			
Labor	_____	_____	_____
Legal fees	_____	_____	_____
Subtotal	_____	_____	_____
4. Test Marketing			
Survey	_____	_____	_____
Number of units	_____	_____	_____
Advertising/publicity	_____	_____	_____
Subtotal	_____	_____	_____
5. Establish Production			
Facilities	_____	_____	_____
Materials	_____	_____	_____
Employees	_____	_____	_____
Subtotal	_____	_____	_____
6. Other	_____	_____	_____
7. Grand Total	_____	_____	_____

Checklist for Selling Invention/Seeking Capital

☐ Made working model

☐ Obtained legal protection

☐ Test-marketed

☐ Prepared business plan

☐ Return on investment projected

☐ Recruited management team

    ☐ President or CEO

    ☐ Accounting

    ☐ Marketing

    ☐ Engineering

☐ Surveyed manufacturers

☐ Surveyed capital sources

☐ Letter requesting appointment for presentation

    ☐ 1st presentation

    ☐ 2nd presentation

    ☐ 3rd presentation

☐ Phone call confirming appointment

    ☐ 1st presentation

    ☐ 2nd presentation

    ☐ 3rd presentation

Checklist for Selling Invention/Seeking Capital

Personal Presentation Notes

a. Advantages of my invention:

_____

_____

_____

_____

_____

b. Anticipation of possible questions:

_____

_____

_____

_____

_____

c. Profit potential:

_____

_____

_____

_____

_____

d. Demonstration:

_____

_____

_____

_____

_____

e. Trial presentation (rehearsal):

_____

_____

_____

_____

_____

Funding Sources and Results

1. Relatives/Friends

a. Name _____ Response _____

_____

b. Name _____ Response _____

_____

c. Name _____ Response _____

_____

d. Name _____ Response _____

_____

e. Name _____ Response _____

_____

2. Banks

a. Name _____ Response _____

_____

b. Name _____ Response _____

_____

c. Name _____ Response _____

_____

d. Name _____ Response _____

_____

e. Name _____ Response _____

_____

Funding Sources and Results

3. Government Programs

a. Name _____   Response _____

_____

b. Name _____   Response _____

_____

c. Name _____   Response _____

_____

d. Name _____   Response _____

_____

e. Name _____   Response _____

_____

4. Venture Capital Companies

a. Name _____   Response _____

_____

b. Name _____   Response _____

_____

c. Name _____   Response _____

_____

d. Name _____   Response _____

_____

e. Name _____   Response _____

_____

III

Glossary

I n Section A, we provide a glossary of words used to describe parts and functions of inventions. In Section B we provide a glossary of patent terms and their definitions as used in patent law.

A. Useful Words to Describe Inventions

This Glossary provides a list of useful words to describe the hardware, parts, and functions of your invention in the specification and claims. The most esoteric of these words are briefly defined. Because of space limitations some definitions are similar; however, all words have nuances in meanings.

If you're looking for a word to describe a certain part, look through the list for a likely prospect and then check a dictionary for its precise meaning. If you can't find the right word here, look in your search patents, in *What's What* or another visual dictionary, or in a thesaurus. If you can't find an appropriate word, you'll probably be able to get away with "member" or "means-plus-a-function" language. Also, for new fields, you may invent words, preferably using Latin or Greek roots, as Farnsworth did with "television," or by extending the meaning of words from analogous devices (e.g., "base" for a part of a transistor). Very technical or specialized fields have their own vocabulary (e.g., "catamenial" in medicine, "syzygy" in astronomy); look in appropriate tutorial texts for these. The words are grouped loosely by the following functions:

1. Structure
2. Mounting & Fastening
3. Springs
4. Numbers
5. Placement
6. Voids
7. Shape
8. Materials & Properties
9. Optics
10. Fluid Flow
11. Electronics
12. Movement
13. Rotation/Machine

1. Structure

annulus (ring)

apron

arbor (shaft)

arm

bail (arch wire)

band

barrel

bascale (seesaw)

base

beam

—cantilever

—simple

belt

bib

blade

blower

board

body

boom

boss (projection)

bougie (body-insertion member)

boule (pear-shaped)

branch

breech (back part)

canard (front wing)

carriage

case

chord

cincture (encircling band)

clew (sail part)

column

configuration

container

conveyor

cornice (horiz. top of structure)

cover

cylinder

dasher (plunger, churn)

detent

device

die

disparate (dissimilar)

diversion

doctor blade (scraper)

dog (holder)

drum

echelon (staggered line)

element

enclosure

fence (stop on tool)

fillet (narrow strip)

fin

finger

finial

flange

fluke (triangular part)

flute (groove on shaft)

frame

fret

frit (vitreous substance)

frustrum (cut-off area)

furcate (branch)

futtock (curved ship timber)

gauge

generatrix (path traced)

gnomon (sundial upright)

grommet

gudgeon (pivot)

gusset (triangular insert)

handle

head

header (base, support)

homologous

housing

hub

jacket

jaw

jib (crane arm)

lagging (support)

leg

lip

list (margin strip)

lobe

magazine

mandrel (tapered axle)

manifold

marginate (w/margin)

medium

member

mullion (dividing strip)

nacelle (pod)

neck

object

outcrop

panel

particle

partition

piece

piston

placket (slit in garment)

platform

plug

plunger

pontoon

portion

post

projection

purlin (horiz. rafter support)

putlog (horiz. support above
  ledger)

pylon (support)

rib

ring

rod

sash (frame)

screed (guide strip)

scroll

sear (catch)

shell

shoe

shoulder

skeleton

sleeve

snorkel

snare

spar (pole support)

spline (projection on shaft)

spoke

sprag (spoke stop)

spur

stanchion

station

stay

stem

stent (stretcher)

  step

  stepped

stile (dividing strip)

stop

strake (ship plank)

strip

strut

tang (shank, tool)

tine

tip

tongue

trace (pivoted rod)

tracery (scrolling)

track

trave (crossbar)

truss

tuft

turret

tuyere (air pipe)

upright

volar (palm, sole)

wall

warp

woof (weft)

2. Mounting & Fastening

attach

billet (tip of belt)

bolt

bonnet

busing

cable

clamp

cleat (reinforcer)

clevis (U-shaped pin)

connection

couple

coupling

cribbing (support)

demountably

docking

dowel

engage

fay (join)

ferrule (barrel)

ferruminate (attach, solder)

fix

gland (sliding holder)

guy wire

harp (lamp shade support)

hold

holder

hook

imbricate (regular overlap)

joint

  —universal

keeper

key

latch

lock

lug

matrix

mount

nail

nut

pin

ribband (holds ribs)

rivet

scarf (notched joint)

screw

seam

seat

secure

set

sliding

snare/loop

solder

springably

support

thill (horse joinder stake)

thrust

weld

3. Springs

air

bias

  —element

coil

compressed

elastic

expanded

helical

  —compression

  —tension

leaf
press
relaxed
resitient
springably
torsional
urge

4. Numbers

argument
compound
difference
dividend
divisor
equation
formula
index
lemma
minuend
modulo
multiplicand
multiplicity
multiplier
plurality
power
product
quotient
remainder
subtrahend
variable

5. Placement (Relation)

adjacent
aft
aligned

angle
aposition (facing)
array
attached
axial
bottom
close
complementary
concentric
contiguous
contracted
course
crest
disposed
distal
divided
edge
engaged
evert (inside out)
extended
external
face
fiducial (reference)
film
fore
horizontal
integral
intermediate
internal
interposed
juxtaposed
layer
located
lower
mating
meshing
mesial (between)
normal
oblique

obtuse
offset
open
opposed
overlapping
parallel
perpendicular
positioned
projecting
prolapsed (out of place)
proximal
proximate
reference
removable
resting
rim
row
sandwich
section
slant
spacer
staggered
superimposed
supported
surface
surrounding
symmetrical
tilt
top
vernier (9:10 gauge)
vertical

6. Voids

aperture
bore
cavity
chamber

concavity

cutout

dimple

duct

embrasure (slant opening)

engraved

filister (groove)

foramen (opening)

fossa (depression)

gain (notch)

gap

groove

hole

hollow

intaglinated (engraved)

lumen (bore of tube)

mortise (cutout)

nock (notch on arrow)

notch

opening

orifice

passage

placket (garment slit)

rabbet (groove)

raceway

recess

separation

slit

slot

sulcus (groove)

ullage (lost liquid)

via (path)

void

7. Shape

acclivity (slope)

acicular (needle-shaped)

agonic (no angle)

annular

anticline (peak)

applanation

arch

arcuate

barrel

bevel

bifurcated (2 branches)

bight (bend)

bucket

buckled

chamfer (beveled)

channel

circular

coin

concave

conical

convex

convoluted (curled in)

corner (inside, outside)

corrugated

crest

crimp

crispate (curled)

cup

cusp (projection)

cylinder

depression

dihedral (two-faced)

direction

disc

dome

drawing (pulling out)

elliptical

fairing (streamlined)

fin

flange

fold

fork

fossa (groove)

fundus (base)

furcate (branched)

helical

hook

incurvate (curved in)

line

lozenge (diamond-shaped)

lune (crescent)

mammilated (nipple-shaped)

notch

oblate (flattened)

oblong

ogive (pointed arch)

orb (globe)

oval

parabolic

parallelogram

plane

prolate (cigar-shaped)

rectangular

reticulated (gridlike)

rhomboid (non-parallel sides)

rhombus (not lozenge)

rick-rock

rill (long narrow valley)

round

salient (standing out)

serrated

setaceous (bristlelike)

sheet

shelf

sinusoidal

slab

spherical

spica (overlapping reverse
   spirals)

square

stamped
striated (grooved
  or ridged)
swaged (flattened)
swale (depression)
syncline (V-shaped)
taper terminus (end)
tesselated (tiled)
topology (unchangeable
  geometry)
tram (on wheels)
trefoil (three-leaved)
triangular
trihedral (3-sided)
trough
tubular
tumescence
  (detumescence)
turbinate (top/spiral-shaped)
twist
upset (distorted)
vermiculate (worm-eaten)
volute (spiral)
wafer
web
wedge
xyresic (razor-sharp)

8. Materials & Properties

adhesive
concrete
cork
dappled (spotted)
denier (gauge)
dense
elastic
enlarged

fabric
fiber
flexible
foraminous
haptic (sense of touch)
humectant (moistener)
insulation
liquid
material
metal
nappy
opaque
pied (splotched)
plastic
porous
prill (pure metal)
refractory
resilient
rigid
rubber
sand
screen
shirred (gathered)
smectic (cleaning)
stratified (layered)
strong
sturdy
translucent
transparent
wood
xerotic (dry)

9. Optics

astigmatic
bezel
bulb
  —fluorescent

—incandescent
fresnel
lamp
light
  —beam
  —ray
opaque
pellicle
pellucid (clear)
reflection
refraction
schlieren (streaks)
translucent
transmission
transparent
window

10. Fluid Flow

accumulator
afferent (to center)
aspirator
bellows
bibb (valve)
bung (hole or stopper)
cock (valve)
conduit
connector
convection
cylinder
  —piston
  —rod
dashpot
diaphragm
discharge
dispenser
efferent (away from center)
filter

fitting

flue

gasket

hose

hydraulic

medium

navicular (like boat)

nozzle

obturator (blocker)

outlet

pipe

plunger

poppet (axial valve)

port

—inlet

—outlet

pump

—centrifugal

—gear

—piston

—reservoir

—seal

—siphon

—tank

—vane

sparge (spray)

sprue (vent tube)

tube

valve

—ball

—check

—control

—gate

—shutoff

wattle (intertwined wall)

weir (dam)

wicket (gate or door)

11. Electronics

adder

amplifier

astable

capacitance

clipping

conductor

contact

control element

demodulator

diode

electrode

electromagnet

filament

flip flop

gate (AND, OR, etc.)

impedance

inductance

insulator

integrated circuit

laser

lead

light-emitting diode

line cord

liquid crystal

maser

memory

motor

multiplier

multivibrator

oscillator

pixel (CRT spot)

power supply

raster

read-and-write memory

read-only memory

resistance

sampling

Schmitt trigger

shift register

Shottky diode

socket

solenoid

switch

terminal

thermistor

transformer

transistor

triode

valve

varistor

wire

Zener diode

12. Movement

alternate

articulate (jointed)

avulsion (tear away)

cam

compression

cyclic

detent (click)

downward

draft (pull)

drag

drift pin

drill

eccentric

emergent

epicyclic (on circle)

escape(ment)

extensible

extrude

grinding

impact

inclined plane

inertia

interval

lag

lead

lever

linkage

  —parallel

longitudinal

machine

meeting

nutate (to and fro)

pressing

propelling

pulverize

sagging

sequacious (regular)

severing

skive (peel)

slidable

straight line

  —motion

snub (stop)

terminating

toggle

torque

traction

transverse

traversing

triturate (grind to powder)

trochoid (roll on circle)

urging

vibrating

wedge

13. Rotation/Machine

antifriction

  —ball

  —needle

  —roller

  —tapered

arbor (shaft)

bell crank

brake

  —band

  —disc

  —shoe

bushing

cam

chain

clevis (circular holder)

clutch

  —centrifugal

  —one-way

  —sprag (stop)

  —toothed

cog (tooth)

connecting rod

crank arm

drive

  —belt

  —pulley

  —sheave

  —toothed

flexible coupling

friction

fulcrum

gear

  —bevel

  —crown

  —internal

  —non-circular

  —pinion

  —right angle

  —spur

  —wheel

  —worm

gin (hoist, pile driver, pump)

guide

intermittent

  —escapement

  —geneva

  —pawl

  —pendulum

  —ratchet

jack

journal

mandrel

orbit

pivot

pulley

radial

radius bar

screw

seal

sheave (pulley)

spindle

sprocket

tappet (valve cam)

variable speed

ward (ridge or notch)

winch

yoke

B. Patent Terms

abstract   A concise, one-paragraph summary of the patent; it details the structure, nature and purpose of the invention. The abstract is used by the PTO and the public to determine quickly the gist of what is being disclosed.

answer   a written response to a complaint (the opening papers in a lawsuit) in which the defendant admits or denies the allegations and provides a list of defenses.

best mode   The inventor's principal and preferred method of embodying the invention.

Board of Appeals and Patent Interferences (BAPI)   A tribunal of judges at the PTO that hears appeals from final office actions.

cease and desist letter   Correspondence from the owner of a proprietary work that requests the cessation of all infringing activity.

clear and convincing proof   Evidence that is highly probable and free from serious doubt.

complaint   an initial document filed in a lawsuit that names the parties and states the conduct performed by the defendant for which it should be held liable to the plaintiff.

compositions of matter   Items such as chemical compositions, conglomerates, aggregates, or other chemically significant substances that are usually supplied in bulk (solid or particulate), liquid, or gaseous form.

conception   The mental part of inventing, how an invention is formulated or how a problem is solved.

confidentiality agreement (also known as a **non-disclosure agreement**)   A contract in which one or both parties agree not to disclose certain information.

continuation application   A new patent application that allows the applicant to re-present an invention and get a second or third bite at the apple. The applicant can file a new application (known as a "continuation") while the original (or "parent") application is still pending. A continuation application consists of the same invention, cross-referenced to the parent application and a new set of claims. The applicant retains the filing date of the parent application for purposes of determining the relevancy of prior art.

continuation-in-part (CIP)   Less common than a continuation application, this form of extension application is used when a portion or all of an earlier patent application is continued and new matter (not disclosed in the earlier application) is included. CIP applications are used when an applicant wants to present an improvement but is prevented from adding it to a pending application because of the prohibition against adding "new matter."

Continuing Prosecution Application (CPA)   A patent application that is like a continuation application in effect, but no new application need be filed. The applicant merely pays another filing fee, submits new claims and files a CPA request form. CPAs can only be used for applications filed prior to 2000 May 29. Applications after that date must use the Request for Continued Examination.

contributory infringement   Occurs when a material component of a patented invention is sold with knowledge that the component is designed for an unauthorized use; cannot occur unless there is a direct infringement. In other words, it is not enough to sell infringing parts; those parts must be used in an infringing invention.

copyright The legal right to exclude others, for a limited time, from copying, selling, performing, displaying, or making derivative versions of a work of authorship such as writing, music, or artwork.

counterclaim A claim for relief usually asserted by the defendant against an opposing party, usually the plaintiff.

Court of Appeals for the Federal Circuit (CAFC) The federal appeals court that specializes in patent appeals. If the Board of Appeals and Patent Interferences rejects an application appeal, applicant can further appeal to the CAFC within 60 days of the decision. If the CAFC upholds the PTO, the applicant can request the United States Supreme Court hear the case (although the Supreme Court rarely hears patent appeals).

date of invention The earliest of the following dates: (a) the date an inventor filed the patent application (provisional or regular); (b) the date an inventor can prove that the invention was built and tested in the U.S. or a country that is a member of the North American Free Trade Association (NAFTA) or the World Trade Organization (WTO); or (c) the date an inventor can prove that the invention was conceived in a NAFTA or WTO country, provided the inventor can also prove diligence in building and testing it, or filing a patent application on it.

declaratory relief request that the court sort out the rights and legal obligations of the parties in the midst of an actual controversy.

deposit date The date of receipt by the PTO of a patent application.

deposition oral or written testimony of a party or witness and given under oath.

design patent Covers the unique, ornamental, or visible shape or design of a non-natural object.

divisional application A patent application used when an applicant wants to protect several inventions claimed in the original application. The official definition is "a later application for a distinct or independent invention, carved out of a pending application and disclosing and claiming only subject matter disclosed in the earlier or parent application" (MPEP 201.06). A divisional application is entitled to the filing date of the parent case for purposes of overcoming prior art. The divisional application must be filed while the parent is pending. A divisional application can be filed as a CPA, q.v.

doctrine of equivalents (DoE.) A form of patent infringement that occurs when an invention performs substantially the same function in substantially the same manner and obtains the same result as the patented invention. A court analyzes each element of the patented invention separately. Under a recent Supreme Court decision, the DoE. must be applied on an element-by-element basis to the claims.

double patenting When an applicant has obtained a patent and has filed a second application containing the same invention, the second application will be rejected, or if the second application resulted in a patent, that patent will be invalidated. Two applications contain the same invention when the two inventions are literally the same, or the second invention is an obvious modification of the first invention.

enhanced damages (treble damages) In exceptional infringement cases, financial damages may be increased, at the discretion of the court, up to triple the award (known as "enhanced damages").

exclusive jurisdiction   The sole authority of a court to hear a certain type of case.

exhaustion (see **first sale doctrine**)

experimental use doctrine   A rule excusing an inventor from the one-year bar provided that the alleged sale or public use was primarily for the purpose of perfecting or testing the invention.

file wrapper estoppel (or **prosecution history estoppel**)   Affirmative defense used in patent infringement litigation that precludes a patent owner from asserting rights that were disclaimed during the patent application process. Term is derived from the fact that the official file in which a patent is contained at the Patent and Trademark Office is known as a "file wrapper." All statements, admissions, correspondence, or documentation relating to the invention are placed in the file wrapper. Estoppel means that a party is prevented from contradicting a former statement or action.

final office action   The examiner's response to the applicant's first amendment. The final office action is supposed to end the prosecution stage, but a "final action" is rarely final.

first office action (sometimes called an **official letter** or **OA**)   Response from the patent examiner after the initial examination of the application. It is very rare that an application is allowed in the first office action. More often, the examiner rejects some or all of the claims.

first sale doctrine (also known as the **exhaustion doctrine**)   Once a patented product (or product resulting from a patented process) is sold or licensed, the patent owner's rights are exhausted and the owner has no further rights as to the resale of that particular article.

indirect infringement   Occurs either when someone is persuaded to make, use, or sell a patented invention without authorization (inducing infringement); or when a material component of a patented invention is sold with knowledge that the component is designed for an unauthorized use (contributory infringement). An indirect infringement cannot occur unless there is a direct infringement. In other words, it is not enough to sell infringing parts; those parts must be used in an infringing invention.

infringement   An invention is infringing if it is a literal copy of a patented invention or if it performs substantially the same function in substantially the same manner and obtains the same result as the patented invention (see "doctrine of equivalents").

injunction   A court order requiring that a party halt a particular activity. In the case of patent infringement, a court can order all infringing activity be halted at the end of a trial (a permanent injunction) or the patent owner can attempt to halt the infringing activity immediately, rather than wait for a trial (a preliminary injunction). Two factors are used when a court determines whether to grant a preliminary injunction: (1) Is the plaintiff likely to succeed in the lawsuit? and (2) Will the plaintiff suffer irreparable harm if the injunction is not granted? The patent owner may seek relief for a very short injunction known as a temporary restraining order (TRO) which is short in duration, usually only a few days or weeks. A temporary restraining order may be granted without notice to the infringer if it appears that immediate damage will result (for example, that evidence will be destroyed).

interference A costly, complex PTO proceeding that determines who will get a patent when two or more applicants are claiming the same invention. It is basically a method of sorting out priority of inventorship. Occasionally an interference may involve a patent that has been in force for less than one year.

interrogatories Written questions that must be answered under oath.

invention Any new article, machine, composition, or process or new use developed by a human.

jury instructions Explanations of the legal rules that the jury shall use in reaching a verdict.

lab notebook A system of documenting invention that usually includes: descriptions of the invention and novel features, procedures used in the building and testing of invention, drawings, photos, or sketches of the invention, test results and conclusions, discussions of any known prior-art references, and additional documentation such as correspondence and purchase receipts.

literal infringement Occurs if a defendant makes, sells, or uses the invention defined in the plaintiff's patent claim. In other words, the infringing machine includes each and every component, part or step in the patented invention. It is a literal infringement because the defendant's device is actually the same invention in the patent claim.

machine A device or things used for accomplishing a task; usually involves some activity or motion performed by working parts.

magistrate An officer of the court, who may exercise some of the authority of a federal district court judge including the authority to conduct a jury or non jury trial.

manufactures (sometimes termed **articles of manufacture**) Items that have been made by human hands or by machines; may have working or moving parts as prime features.

means-plus-function clause (or **means for clause**) A provision in a patent claim in which the applicant may not specifically describe the structure of one of the items in the patent and instead describes the function of the item. Term is derived from the fact that the clause usually starts with the word "means."

new matter Any technical information, including dimensions, materials, etc., that was not present in the patent application as originally filed. An applicant can never add new matter to an application (PTO Rule 118).

new-use invention A new and unobvious process or method for using an old and known invention.

nonobviousness A standard of patentability that requires that an invention produce "unusual and surprising results." In 1966, the U.S. Supreme Court established the steps for determining unobviousness in the case of Graham v. John Deere.

Notice of Allowance Document issued when the examiner is convinced that the application meets the requirements of patentability. An issue fee is due within three months.

objects and advantages The term "objects" refers to "what the invention accomplishes." Usually, the objects are also the invention's advantages, since those aspects are intended to be superior over prior art.

on-sale bar Prevents an inventor from acquiring patent protection if the application is filed more than one year from the date of sale, use, or offer of sale of the invention in the United States.

one-year rule An inventor must file a patent application within one year after selling, offering for sale, or commercially or publicly using or describing an invention. If an inventor fails to file within one year of such occurrence, the inventor is barred from obtaining a patent.

patent A grant from a government that confers upon an inventor the right to exclude others from making, using, selling, importing, or offering an invention for sale for a fixed period of time.

patent application A set of papers that describe an invention and that are suitable for filing in a patent office in order to apply for a patent on the invention.

Patent Application Declaration (PAD) The declaration identifies the inventor or joint inventors and provides an attestation by the applicant that the inventor understands the contents of the claims and specification and has fully disclosed all material information. The PTO provides a form for the PAD.

patent misuse A defense in patent infringement that prevents a patent owner who has abused patent law from enforcing patent rights. Common examples of misuse are violation of the antitrust laws or unethical business practices.

patent pending (also known as the **pendency period**) Period between when a patent application (or PPA) is filed and the patent is issued. The inventor has no patent rights during this period. However, when and if the patent later issues, the inventor will obtain the right to prevent the continuation of any infringing activity that started during the pendency period. If the application has been published by the PTO during the pendency period and the infringer had notice, the applicant may later seek royalties for these infringements during the pendency period. It's a criminal offense to use the words "patent applied for" or "patent pending" (they mean the same thing) in any advertising when there's no active, applicable regular or provisional patent application on file.

patent prosecution The process of shepherding a patent application through the Patent and Trademark Office.

Patent Rules of Practice Administrative regulations located in Volume 37 of the Code of Federal Regulations (37 CFR § 1).

pendency period (see **patent pending**)

permanent injunction A durable injunction issued after a final judgment on the merits of the case; permanently restrains the defendant from engaging in the infringing activity.

Petition to Make Special An applicant can, under certain circumstances, have an application examined sooner than the normal course of PTO examination (one to three years). This is accomplished by filing a "Petition to Make Special" (PTMS), together with a Supporting Declaration.

plant patent Covers plants that can be reproduced through the use of grafts and cuttings (asexually reproducible), such as flowers.

power of attorney Only an inventor, a patent agent, or a patent attorney may prepare and file a patent application. If an attorney is preparing an application on behalf of an inventor, a power of attorney should be executed to authorize the patent attorney or agent to act on behalf of the inventor. The power of attorney form may be combined with the PAD.

preponderance of evidence   Proof which produces the belief that the facts are more likely true than not true.

prior art   The state of knowledge existing or publicly available either before the date of an invention or more than one year prior to the patent application date.

Provisional patent application (PPA) an interim document that clearly explains how to make and use the invention and is equivalent to a reduction to practice. If a regular patent application is filed within one year of filing the PPA, the inventor can use the PPA's filing date for the purpose of deciding whether a reference is prior art. In addition to an early filing date, an inventor may claim patent pending status for the one-year period following the filing of PPA.

process (sometimes referred to as a **method**)   A way of doing or making things that involves more than purely mental manipulations.

reduction to practice   The point at which the inventor can demonstrate that the invention works for its intended purpose. Reduction to practice can be accomplished by building and testing the invention (**actual reduction to practice**) or by preparing a patent application or provisional patent application that shows how to make and use the invention and that it works (**constructive reduction practice**). In the event of a dispute or a challenge at the PTO, invention documentation is essential in proving the "how and when" of conception and reduction to practice.

reissue application   An application used to correct information in a patent. It is usually filed when a patent owner believes the claims are not broad enough, the claims are too broad (the applicant discovered a new reference), or there are significant errors in the specification. In these cases, the applicant seeks to correct the patent by filing an application to get the applicant's original patent reissued at any time during its term. The reissue patent will take the place of the applicant's original patent and expire at the same time the original patent would have expired. If the applicant wants to broaden the claims of the patent through a reissue application, the applicant must do so within two years from the date the original patent issued. There is a risk in filing a reissue application because all of the claims of the original patent will be examined and can be rejected.

repair doctrine   Affirmative defense based on the right of an authorized licensor of a patented device to repair and replace unpatented components. It also includes the right to sell materials used to repair or replace a patented invention.

request for admission   Request for a party to the lawsuit to admit the truthfulness of a fact or statement.

Request for Continued Examination (RCE) A paper filed when a patent applicant wishes to continue prosecuting an application that has received a final action. Filing the RCE with another filing fee effectively removes the final action so that the applicant can submit further amendments, e.g., new claims, new arguments, a new declaration, new references, etc., as if the final action were a non-final action.

request for production of documents   Method by which a party to the lawsuit may obtain documents or other physical evidence.

reverse doctrine of equivalents (or **negative doctrine of equivalents**)   A rarely used affirmative defense to patent infringement in which, even if there is a literal infringement, the court will excuse the defendant's conduct if the infringing device has a different function or result than the patented invention. In other words, the allegedly infringing device performs the same function in a substantially different way.

sequence listing   If a biotech invention includes a sequence listing of a nucleotide or amino acid sequence, the applicant attaches this information on separate sheets of paper and references the sequence listing in the application (see PTO Rule 77). If there is no sequence listing, the applicant states "Non applicable."

small entity declaration (SED)   In order to encourage inventors, fees are reduced for small business, independent inventors, and nonprofit companies. To qualify, the applicant must file a verified statement declaring that no "large entity" has any rights in the invention. This is commonly done at the time of filing, or may be done any time within 60 days of payment of the reduced fee. There are three types of small entities: (1) independent inventors; (2) nonprofit companies; and (3) small businesses. To qualify, an independent inventor must either own all rights, or have transferred—or be obligated to transfer—rights to a small business or nonprofit organization. Nonprofit organizations are defined and listed in the Code of Federal Regulations and usually are educational institutions or charitable organizations. A small entity business is one with less than 500 employees. The number of employees is computed by averaging the number of full- and part-time employees during a fiscal year.

specification   Patent application disclosure by inventor; drafted so that an individual skilled in the art to which the invention pertains could, when reading the patent, make and use the invention without the necessity of further experiment.

statute of limitations   There is no time limit (statute of limitations) for filing a patent infringement lawsuit, but monetary damages can only be recovered for infringements committed during the six years prior to filing the lawsuit. For example, if a patent owner sues after ten years of infringement, the owner cannot recover monetary damages for the first four years of infringement. Despite the fact that there is no law setting a time limit, courts will not permit a patent owner to sue for infringement if the owner has waited an unreasonable time to file the lawsuit ("laches").

Statutory Invention Registration (SIR)   A Statutory Invention Registration allows an applicant who abandons an application to prevent anyone else from getting a valid patent on the same invention. This is accomplished by converting the patent application to a SIR.

statutory subject matter   An invention that falls into one of the five statutory classes: process (method), machine, article of manufacture, composition, or a "new use" of one of the first four.

substitute application   Essentially a duplicate of an abandoned patent application. (See MPEP 201.09.) The disadvantage of a substitute application is that the applicant doesn't get the benefit of the filing date of the previously abandoned patent application.

Any prior art occurring after the filing date of the earlier case can be used against the substitute case. If the applicant's substitute application issues into a patent, the patent will expire 20 years from the filing date of the substitute.

successor liability When a company is liable for infringement because it has purchased another company liable for infringements.

summons a document served with the complaint that explains that the defendant has been sued and has a certain time limit in which to respond.

temporary restraining order (TRO) an injunction, often granted *ex parte*, that is short in duration and only remains in effect until the court has an opportunity to schedule a hearing for the preliminary injunction.

tying A form of patent misuse in which, as a condition of a transaction, the buyer of a patented device must also purchase an additional product. For example, in one case a company had a patent on a machine that deposited salt tablets in canned food. Purchasers of the machine were also required to buy salt tablets from the patent owner.

utility patent The main type of patent; covers inventions that function in a unique manner to produce a utilitarian result.

vicarious liability When a business such as a corporation or partnership is liable for infringements committed by employees or agents.

voir dire *("speak the truth")* Process by which attorneys question potential jurors. ∎

IV

Fee Schedule

PTO Fees (Rule)

For current Fee Information, check the PTO website (http://www.uspto.gov)

Service or Item	Fee ($)

Disclosure Document, filing (21(c)) 10

Provisional Patent Appn., Filing 150/75

Printed Copy of Patent or Patent
  Order Coupon Utility/Design;
  Also for Copy of SIR (19(a)) 3

Copy of Patent With Color Drawings (19(a)) 25

Application Filing Fees:

Utility Patent (incl. reissue) (16(a)) 740/370

Design Patent (16(f)) 330/165

Plant Patent (16(g)) 510/255

Fee for Each Independent Claim
  Over Three (16(b)) 84/42

Fee for Each Claim Over Twenty
  (Independent or Dependent) (16(c)) 18/9

Surcharge—Multiple Dependent
  Claims in Any Application (16(d)) 280/140

Surcharge If Filing Fee or
  Declaration Late (16(e)) 130/65

Recording Assignment per Application
  or Patent Involved (21(h)) 40

Surcharge If Any Check Bounces (21(m)) 50

Petitions to Commissioner:

Regarding Inventorship, Misc.,
  Maint. Fees, Interferences, Foreign
  Filing Licenses, Access to Records,
  Foreign Priority Papers, Amendments
  After Issue Fee, Defer/Withdraw a
  Case From Issue (17(k,l)) 130

To Make Application Special (17(l)) 130

In a PPA, to correct inventorship,
  convert an RPA to a PPA, and accord
  a PPA a filing date (17(a)) 50

Service or Item	Fee ($)

Extensions to Reply to Office Action:

1st Month (17(a)) 110/55

2nd Month (17(b)) 400/200

3rd Month (17(c)) 920/460

4th Month (if available) (17(d)) 1,440/720

Petition to Revive Abandoned Appn.:

  Unavoidable Delay (17(l)) 110/55

  Unintentional Delay (17(m)) 1,280/640

Certified Copy Patent Application
  as Filed (19(b)) 15

Appeal to Board of Appeals & Pat. Intrfs.:

Filing Notice of Appeal (17(b)) 320/160

Filing Brief (17(c)) 320/160

Oral Hearing (17(g)) 280/140

Application Issue Fees:

Utility Patent (18(a)) 1,280/640

Design Patent (18(b)) 460/230

Plant Patent (18(c)) 620/310

Certificate to Correct Patent
  (Applicant's Mistake) (20(a)) 100

Re-examination Fee (20(c)) 2,520

PTO Fees (Rule) (continued)

Service or Item	Fee ($)

Utility Patent Maintenance Fees:

I (3.5 years—pays for yrs 4 thru 8)
(20(e)) 880/440

II (7.5 years—pays for yrs 9 thru 12)
(20(f)) 2,020/1010

III (11.5 years—pays for yrs 13 thru 17)
(20(g)) 3,100/1,550

Late Charge (in 6-month grace period)
(20(h)) 130/65

Petition to Revive (after patent expires)
—unintentional delay (20(i)) 1,640

Petition to Revive (after patent expires)
—unavoidable delay (20(i)) 700

Other Fees

Service or Item	Fee ($)

Certified Copy of File & Contents
—Issued Patent (19(b)(2)) 200

Certified Copy of Patent
Assignment Record (19(b)(3)) 25

Disclaimer of Claims or Terminal
Part of Term of Patent (20(d)) 110/55

Dedication of Entire Term or
Terminal Part of Term of Patent...................... NC

Trademark Application Filing (in PTO) 325

Copyright Application Filing
(in Copyright Office) 30

PCT Fees

Service or Item	Fee ($)

(Always check just before filing; these fees change frequently)

Transmittal Fee 240

Search Fees:

In U.S. PTO

—no corres. prior U.S. appn. filed 700

—corres. prior U.S. appn. filed 450

International Fees:

Basic (First 30 Pages) 407

Each Additional Sheet Over 30 9

Designation Fee, each country or
office up to 10 88

11th and additional countries or offices .... NC

Chapter II Fees:

Handling Fee 146

Examination Fee

In U.S. PTO (assuming a patent search
is done by the U.S. PTO, as described
in Chapter 1) 450

■

V

Tear-Out Forms

n Appendix V we provide you with tear-out copies of the following:

- Consultant's Work Agreement. If you do use a consultant (for example, a model maker) you should take precautions to protect the confidentiality and proprietary status of your invention. There's no substitute for checking out your consultant carefully by asking for references (assuming you don't already know the consultant). In addition, have your consultant sign a copy of the Consultant's Work Agreement. For more information on this subject, see Chapter 4 of *Patent It Yourself.*

- Proprietary Materials Agreement. This agreement is designed for use when you disclose significant details about an unpatented invention to potential developers, investors, evaluators, or partners. The form binds the recipient of the information to confidentiality so you can preserve your invention as a trade secret up until the time your patent is made public.

- Joint Owners' Agreement. Problems commonly arise in situations where there are two or more inventors or owners of a patent application or patent. These include questions as to who is entitled to commercially exploit the invention, financial shares, what type of accounting must be performed on partnership books, etc. Fortunately, most of these problems can be eliminated by the use of a Joint Owners' Agreement (JOA). More information on joint ownership issues is available in Chapter 16 of *Patent It Yourself.*

- Assignment of Invention and Patent Application. To make a transfer of ownership in the arcane patent world, you must sign an "assignment"—a legal document that the law will recognize as effective to make the transfer of ownership. An assignment for transferring ownership of an invention is provided. A cover sheet and fee must be submitted to the PTO with any assignment to be recorded. More information about this procedure and about assignment of patent rights is available in Chapter 16 of *Patent It Yourself.* The assignment document presented here, like the Joint Owners' Agreement, is but one of many possible alternatives. If you use it, you may want to change a number of provisions to fit your situation. Also, keep in mind, a consultation with a patent attorney is advisable if you wish to fully understand how this agreement will affect your rights.

- Universal License Agreement. This agreement can be used to exclusively or nonexclusively license your invention as well as to license know-how. It can also be used to grant a potential licensee an option to evaluate your invention for a given period in return for a payment. Most companies will either prefer to use their own license agreement or to make one up from scratch, but you can use the Universal License Agreement for purposes of comparison.

- Request for Participation in Disclosure Document Program. This is a cover letter for filing an Invention Disclosure. (See Chapter 2, Section C, of this book or Chapter 3 of *Patent it Yourself.*)

- Invention Disclosure Statement. This form is used to document conception when filing under the Disclosure Document Program. (See Chapter 2, Section C, of this book or Chapter 3 of *Patent it Yourself.*)

- Provisional Patent Application Cover Letter. This is a cover letter for filing a provisional patent application (See Chapter 2, Section E, of this book or Chapter 3 of *Patent it Yourself.*)

Consultant's Work Agreement

1. **Parties:** This Work Agreement is made between the following parties:

   Name(s): _____

   Address(es): _____

   _____

   (hereinafter Contractor), and

   Name(s): _____

   Address(es): _____

   _____

   (hereinafter Consultant).

2. **Name of Project:**

   _____

   _____

3. **Work to Be Performed by Consultant:**

   _____

   _____

4. **Work/Payment Schedule:**

   _____

   _____

5. **Date:** This Agreement shall be effective as of the latter date below written.

6. **Recitals:** Contractor has one or more ideas relating to the above project and desires to have such project developed more completely, as specified in the above statement of Work. Consultant has certain skills desired by Contractor relating to performance of the above Work.

7. **Performance:** Consultant will perform the above work for Contractor in accordance with the above-scheduled Work/Payment Schedule, and Contractor will make the above-scheduled payments to Consultant. Any changes to the Work to Be Performed or the Work/Payment Schedule shall be described in a writing referring to this Agreement and signed and dated by both parties. Time is of the essence of this Agreement, and if Consultant fails to perform according to the above work schedule, contractor may (a) void this agreement and pay consultant 50% of what would otherwise be due, or (b) require that Consultant pay contractor a penalty of $_____ per day.

8. **Intellectual Property:** All intellectual property, including trademarks, writings, information, trade secrets, inventions, discoveries, or improvements, whether or not registrable or patentable, which are conceived, constructed, or written by Consultant and arise out of or are related to work and services performed under this agreement, are, or shall become and remain the sole and exclusive property of Contractor, whether or not such intellectual property is conceived during the time such work and services are performed or billed.

9A. **Protection of Intellectual Property:** Contractor and Consultant recognize that under U.S. patent laws, all patent applications must be filed in the name of the true and actual inventor(s) of the subject matter sought to be patented. Thus if Consultant makes any patentable inventions relating to the above project, Consultant agrees to be named as an applicant in any U.S. patent application(s) filed on such invention(s). Actual ownership of such patent applications shall be governed by clause 8.

9B. Consultant shall promptly disclose to Contractor in writing all information pertaining to any intellectual property generated or conceived by Consultant under this Agreement. Consultant hereby assigns and agrees to assign all of Consultant's rights to such intellectual property, including patent rights and foreign priority rights. Consultant hereby expressly agrees, without further charge for time, to do all things and sign all documents deemed by Contractor to be necessary or appropriate to invest in intellectual property, including obtaining for and vesting in Contractor all U.S. and foreign patents and patent applications which Contractor desires to obtain to cover such intellectual property, provided that Contractor shall bear all expenses relating thereto. All reasonable local travel time and expenses shall be borne by Consultant.

10. **Trade Secrets:** Consultant recognizes that all information relating to the above Project disclosed to Consultant by Contractor, and all information generated by Consultant in the performance of the above Work, is a valuable trade secret of Contractor and Consultant shall treat all such information as strictly confidential, during and after the performance of Work under this Agreement. Specifically Consultant shall not reveal, publish, or communicate any such information to anyone other than Contractor, and shall safeguard all such information from access to anyone other than Contractor, except upon the express written authorization of Contractor. This clause shall not apply to any information which Consultant can document in writing is presently in or enters the public domain from a bona fide source other than Consultant.

11. **Return of Property:** Consultant agrees to return all written materials and objects received from Contractor, to deliver to Contractor all objects and a copy (and all copies and originals if requested by Contractor) of all written materials resulting from or relating to work performed under this Agreement, and not to deliver to any person, organization, or publisher, or cause to be published, any such written material without prior written authorization.

12. **Conflicts of Interest:** Consultant recognizes a fiduciary obligation to Contractor arising out of the work and services performed under this agreement and accordingly will not offer Consultant's service to or perform services for any competitor, potential or actual, of Contractor for the above Project, or perform any other acts which may result in any conflict of interest by Consultant, during and after the term of this Agreement.

13. **Mediation and Arbitration:** If any dispute arises under this Agreement, the parties shall negotiate in good faith to settle such dispute. If the parties cannot resolve such dispute themselves, then either party may submit the dispute to mediation by a mediator approved by both parties. If the parties cannot agree to any mediator, or if either party does not wish to abide by any decision of the mediator, they shall submit the dispute to arbitration by any mutually acceptable arbitrator, or the American Arbitration Association (AAA). If the AAA is selected, the arbitration shall take place under the auspices of the nearest branch of such to both parties. The costs of the arbitration proceeding shall be borne according to the decision of the arbitrator, who may apportion costs equally, or in accordance with any finding or fault or lack of good faith of either party. The arbitrator's award shall be nonappealable and enforceable in any court of competent jurisdiction.

14. **Governing Law:** This Agreement shall be governed by and interpreted under and according to the laws of the State of _____.

15. **Signatures:** The parties have indicated their agreement to all of the above terms by signing this Agreement on the respective dates below indicated. Each party has received an original signed copy hereof.

Contractor: _____ Date: _____

Consultant: _____ Date: _____

Consultant's Work Agreement

1. **Parties:** This Work Agreement is made between the following parties:

   Name(s): _____

   Address(es): _____

   _____

   (hereinafter Contractor), and

   Name(s): _____

   Address(es): _____

   _____

   (hereinafter Consultant).

2. **Name of Project:**

   _____

   _____

3. **Work to Be Performed by Consultant:**

   _____

   _____

4. **Work/Payment Schedule:**

   _____

   _____

5. **Date:** This Agreement shall be effective as of the latter date below written.

6. **Recitals:** Contractor has one or more ideas relating to the above project and desires to have such project developed more completely, as specified in the above statement of Work. Consultant has certain skills desired by Contractor relating to performance of the above Work.

7. **Performance:** Consultant will perform the above work for Contractor in accordance with the above-scheduled Work/Payment Schedule, and Contractor will make the above-scheduled payments to Consultant. Any changes to the Work to Be Performed or the Work/Payment Schedule shall be described in a writing referring to this Agreement and signed and dated by both parties. Time is of the essence of this Agreement, and if Consultant fails to perform according to the above work schedule, contractor may (a) void this agreement and pay consultant 50% of what would otherwise be due, or (b) require that Consultant pay contractor a penalty of $_____ per day.

8. **Intellectual Property:** All intellectual property, including trademarks, writings, information, trade secrets, inventions, discoveries, or improvements, whether or not registrable or patentable, which are conceived, constructed, or written by Consultant and arise out of or are related to work and services performed under this agreement, are, or shall become and remain the sole and exclusive property of Contractor, whether or not such intellectual property is conceived during the time such work and services are performed or billed.

9A. **Protection of Intellectual Property:** Contractor and Consultant recognize that under U.S. patent laws, all patent applications must be filed in the name of the true and actual inventor(s) of the subject matter sought to be patented. Thus if Consultant makes any patentable inventions relating to the above project, Consultant agrees to be named as an applicant in any U.S. patent application(s) filed on such invention(s). Actual ownership of such patent applications shall be governed by clause 8.

9B. Consultant shall promptly disclose to Contractor in writing all information pertaining to any intellectual property generated or conceived by Consultant under this Agreement. Consultant hereby assigns and agrees to assign all of Consultant's rights to such intellectual property, including patent rights and foreign priority rights. Consultant hereby expressly agrees, without further charge for time, to do all things and sign all documents deemed by Contractor to be necessary or appropriate to invest in intellectual property, including obtaining for and vesting in Contractor all U.S. and foreign patents and patent applications which Contractor desires to obtain to cover such intellectual property, provided that Contractor shall bear all expenses relating thereto. All reasonable local travel time and expenses shall be borne by Consultant.

10. **Trade Secrets:** Consultant recognizes that all information relating to the above Project disclosed to Consultant by Contractor, and all information generated by Consultant in the performance of the above Work, is a valuable trade secret of Contractor and Consultant shall treat all such information as strictly confidential, during and after the performance of Work under this Agreement. Specifically Consultant shall not reveal, publish, or communicate any such information to anyone other than Contractor, and shall safeguard all such information from access to anyone other than Contractor, except upon the express written authorization of Contractor. This clause shall not apply to any information which Consultant can document in writing is presently in or enters the public domain from a bona fide source other than Consultant.

11. **Return of Property:** Consultant agrees to return all written materials and objects received from Contractor, to deliver to Contractor all objects and a copy (and all copies and originals if requested by Contractor) of all written materials resulting from or relating to work performed under this Agreement, and not to deliver to any person, organization, or publisher, or cause to be published, any such written material without prior written authorization.

12. **Conflicts of Interest:** Consultant recognizes a fiduciary obligation to Contractor arising out of the work and services performed under this agreement and accordingly will not offer Consultant's service to or perform services for any competitor, potential or actual, of Contractor for the above Project, or perform any other acts which may result in any conflict of interest by Consultant, during and after the term of this Agreement.

13. **Mediation and Arbitration:** If any dispute arises under this Agreement, the parties shall negotiate in good faith to settle such dispute. If the parties cannot resolve such dispute themselves, then either party may submit the dispute to mediation by a mediator approved by both parties. If the parties cannot agree to any mediator, or if either party does not wish to abide by any decision of the mediator, they shall submit the dispute to arbitration by any mutually acceptable arbitrator, or the American Arbitration Association (AAA). If the AAA is selected, the arbitration shall take place under the auspices of the nearest branch of such to both parties. The costs of the arbitration proceeding shall be borne according to the decision of the arbitrator, who may apportion costs equally, or in accordance with any finding or fault or lack of good faith of either party. The arbitrator's award shall be nonappealable and enforceable in any court of competent jurisdiction.

14. **Governing Law:** This Agreement shall be governed by and interpreted under and according to the laws of the State of _____.

15. **Signatures:** The parties have indicated their agreement to all of the above terms by signing this Agreement on the respective dates below indicated. Each party has received an original signed copy hereof.

Contractor: _____ Date: _____

Consultant: _____ Date: _____

Consultant's Work Agreement

1. **Parties:** This Work Agreement is made between the following parties:

   Name(s): _____

   Address(es): _____

   _____

   (hereinafter Contractor), and

   Name(s): _____

   Address(es): _____

   _____

   (hereinafter Consultant).

2. **Name of Project:**

   _____

   _____

3. **Work to Be Performed by Consultant:**

   _____

   _____

4. **Work/Payment Schedule:**

   _____

   _____

5. **Date:** This Agreement shall be effective as of the latter date below written.

6. **Recitals:** Contractor has one or more ideas relating to the above project and desires to have such project developed more completely, as specified in the above statement of Work. Consultant has certain skills desired by Contractor relating to performance of the above Work.

7. **Performance:** Consultant will perform the above work for Contractor in accordance with the above-scheduled Work/Payment Schedule, and Contractor will make the above-scheduled payments to Consultant. Any changes to the Work to Be Performed or the Work/Payment Schedule shall be described in a writing referring to this Agreement and signed and dated by both parties. Time is of the essence of this Agreement, and if Consultant fails to perform according to the above work schedule, contractor may (a) void this agreement and pay consultant 50% of what would otherwise be due, or (b) require that Consultant pay contractor a penalty of $_____ per day.

8. **Intellectual Property:** All intellectual property, including trademarks, writings, information, trade secrets, inventions, discoveries, or improvements, whether or not registrable or patentable, which are conceived, constructed, or written by Consultant and arise out of or are related to work and services performed under this agreement, are, or shall become and remain the sole and exclusive property of Contractor, whether or not such intellectual property is conceived during the time such work and services are performed or billed.

9A. **Protection of Intellectual Property:** Contractor and Consultant recognize that under U.S. patent laws, all patent applications must be filed in the name of the true and actual inventor(s) of the subject matter sought to be patented. Thus if Consultant makes any patentable inventions relating to the above project, Consultant agrees to be named as an applicant in any U.S. patent application(s) filed on such invention(s). Actual ownership of such patent applications shall be governed by clause 8.

9B. Consultant shall promptly disclose to Contractor in writing all information pertaining to any intellectual property generated or conceived by Consultant under this Agreement. Consultant hereby assigns and agrees to assign all of Consultant's rights to such intellectual property, including patent rights and foreign priority rights. Consultant hereby expressly agrees, without further charge for time, to do all things and sign all documents deemed by Contractor to be necessary or appropriate to invest in intellectual property, including obtaining for and vesting in Contractor all U.S. and foreign patents and patent applications which Contractor desires to obtain to cover such intellectual property, provided that Contractor shall bear all expenses relating thereto. All reasonable local travel time and expenses shall be borne by Consultant.

10. **Trade Secrets:** Consultant recognizes that all information relating to the above Project disclosed to Consultant by Contractor, and all information generated by Consultant in the performance of the above Work, is a valuable trade secret of Contractor and Consultant shall treat all such information as strictly confidential, during and after the performance of Work under this Agreement. Specifically Consultant shall not reveal, publish, or communicate any such information to anyone other than Contractor, and shall safeguard all such information from access to anyone other than Contractor, except upon the express written authorization of Contractor. This clause shall not apply to any information which Consultant can document in writing is presently in or enters the public domain from a bona fide source other than Consultant.

11. **Return of Property:** Consultant agrees to return all written materials and objects received from Contractor, to deliver to Contractor all objects and a copy (and all copies and originals if requested by Contractor) of all written materials resulting from or relating to work performed under this Agreement, and not to deliver to any person, organization, or publisher, or cause to be published, any such written material without prior written authorization.

12. **Conflicts of Interest:** Consultant recognizes a fiduciary obligation to Contractor arising out of the work and services performed under this agreement and accordingly will not offer Consultant's service to or perform services for any competitor, potential or actual, of Contractor for the above Project, or perform any other acts which may result in any conflict of interest by Consultant, during and after the term of this Agreement.

13. **Mediation and Arbitration:** If any dispute arises under this Agreement, the parties shall negotiate in good faith to settle such dispute. If the parties cannot resolve such dispute themselves, then either party may submit the dispute to mediation by a mediator approved by both parties. If the parties cannot agree to any mediator, or if either party does not wish to abide by any decision of the mediator, they shall submit the dispute to arbitration by any mutually acceptable arbitrator, or the American Arbitration Association (AAA). If the AAA is selected, the arbitration shall take place under the auspices of the nearest branch of such to both parties. The costs of the arbitration proceeding shall be borne according to the decision of the arbitrator, who may apportion costs equally, or in accordance with any finding or fault or lack of good faith of either party. The arbitrator's award shall be nonappealable and enforceable in any court of competent jurisdiction.

14. **Governing Law:** This Agreement shall be governed by and interpreted under and according to the laws of the State of _____.

15. **Signatures:** The parties have indicated their agreement to all of the above terms by signing this Agreement on the respective dates below indicated. Each party has received an original signed copy hereof.

Contractor: _____ Date: _____

Consultant: _____ Date: _____

Consultant's Work Agreement

1. **Parties:** This Work Agreement is made between the following parties:

   Name(s): _____

   Address(es): _____

   _____

   (hereinafter Contractor), and

   Name(s): _____

   Address(es): _____

   _____

   (hereinafter Consultant).

2. **Name of Project:**

   _____

   _____

3. **Work to Be Performed by Consultant:**

   _____

   _____

4. **Work/Payment Schedule:**

   _____

   _____

5. **Date:** This Agreement shall be effective as of the latter date below written.

6. **Recitals:** Contractor has one or more ideas relating to the above project and desires to have such project developed more completely, as specified in the above statement of Work. Consultant has certain skills desired by Contractor relating to performance of the above Work.

7. **Performance:** Consultant will perform the above work for Contractor in accordance with the above-scheduled Work/Payment Schedule, and Contractor will make the above-scheduled payments to Consultant. Any changes to the Work to Be Performed or the Work/Payment Schedule shall be described in a writing referring to this Agreement and signed and dated by both parties. Time is of the essence of this Agreement, and if Consultant fails to perform according to the above work schedule, contractor may (a) void this agreement and pay consultant 50% of what would otherwise be due, or (b) require that Consultant pay contractor a penalty of $_____ per day.

8. **Intellectual Property:** All intellectual property, including trademarks, writings, information, trade secrets, inventions, discoveries, or improvements, whether or not registrable or patentable, which are conceived, constructed, or written by Consultant and arise out of or are related to work and services performed under this agreement, are, or shall become and remain the sole and exclusive property of Contractor, whether or not such intellectual property is conceived during the time such work and services are performed or billed.

9A. **Protection of Intellectual Property:** Contractor and Consultant recognize that under U.S. patent laws, all patent applications must be filed in the name of the true and actual inventor(s) of the subject matter sought to be patented. Thus if Consultant makes any patentable inventions relating to the above project, Consultant agrees to be named as an applicant in any U.S. patent application(s) filed on such invention(s). Actual ownership of such patent applications shall be governed by clause 8.

9B. Consultant shall promptly disclose to Contractor in writing all information pertaining to any intellectual property generated or conceived by Consultant under this Agreement. Consultant hereby assigns and agrees to assign all of Consultant's rights to such intellectual property, including patent rights and foreign priority rights. Consultant hereby expressly agrees, without further charge for time, to do all things and sign all documents deemed by Contractor to be necessary or appropriate to invest in intellectual property, including obtaining for and vesting in Contractor all U.S. and foreign patents and patent applications which Contractor desires to obtain to cover such intellectual property, provided that Contractor shall bear all expenses relating thereto. All reasonable local travel time and expenses shall be borne by Consultant.

10. **Trade Secrets:** Consultant recognizes that all information relating to the above Project disclosed to Consultant by Contractor, and all information generated by Consultant in the performance of the above Work, is a valuable trade secret of Contractor and Consultant shall treat all such information as strictly confidential, during and after the performance of Work under this Agreement. Specifically Consultant shall not reveal, publish, or communicate any such information to anyone other than Contractor, and shall safeguard all such information from access to anyone other than Contractor, except upon the express written authorization of Contractor. This clause shall not apply to any information which Consultant can document in writing is presently in or enters the public domain from a bona fide source other than Consultant.

11. **Return of Property:** Consultant agrees to return all written materials and objects received from Contractor, to deliver to Contractor all objects and a copy (and all copies and originals if requested by Contractor) of all written materials resulting from or relating to work performed under this Agreement, and not to deliver to any person, organization, or publisher, or cause to be published, any such written material without prior written authorization.

12. **Conflicts of Interest:** Consultant recognizes a fiduciary obligation to Contractor arising out of the work and services performed under this agreement and accordingly will not offer Consultant's service to or perform services for any competitor, potential or actual, of Contractor for the above Project, or perform any other acts which may result in any conflict of interest by Consultant, during and after the term of this Agreement.

13. **Mediation and Arbitration:** If any dispute arises under this Agreement, the parties shall negotiate in good faith to settle such dispute. If the parties cannot resolve such dispute themselves, then either party may submit the dispute to mediation by a mediator approved by both parties. If the parties cannot agree to any mediator, or if either party does not wish to abide by any decision of the mediator, they shall submit the dispute to arbitration by any mutually acceptable arbitrator, or the American Arbitration Association (AAA). If the AAA is selected, the arbitration shall take place under the auspices of the nearest branch of such to both parties. The costs of the arbitration proceeding shall be borne according to the decision of the arbitrator, who may apportion costs equally, or in accordance with any finding or fault or lack of good faith of either party. The arbitrator's award shall be nonappealable and enforceable in any court of competent jurisdiction.

14. **Governing Law:** This Agreement shall be governed by and interpreted under and according to the laws of the State of _____.

15. **Signatures:** The parties have indicated their agreement to all of the above terms by signing this Agreement on the respective dates below indicated. Each party has received an original signed copy hereof.

Contractor: _____ Date: _____

Consultant: _____ Date: _____

Consultant's Work Agreement

1. **Parties:** This Work Agreement is made between the following parties:

   Name(s): _____

   Address(es): _____

   _____

   (hereinafter Contractor), and

   Name(s): _____

   Address(es): _____

   _____

   (hereinafter Consultant).

2. **Name of Project:**

   _____

   _____

3. **Work to Be Performed by Consultant:**

   _____

   _____

4. **Work/Payment Schedule:**

   _____

   _____

5. **Date:** This Agreement shall be effective as of the latter date below written.

6. **Recitals:** Contractor has one or more ideas relating to the above project and desires to have such project developed more completely, as specified in the above statement of Work. Consultant has certain skills desired by Contractor relating to performance of the above Work.

7. **Performance:** Consultant will perform the above work for Contractor in accordance with the above-scheduled Work/Payment Schedule, and Contractor will make the above-scheduled payments to Consultant. Any changes to the Work to Be Performed or the Work/Payment Schedule shall be described in a writing referring to this Agreement and signed and dated by both parties. Time is of the essence of this Agreement, and if Consultant fails to perform according to the above work schedule, contractor may (a) void this agreement and pay consultant 50% of what would otherwise be due, or (b) require that Consultant pay contractor a penalty of $_____ per day.

8. **Intellectual Property:** All intellectual property, including trademarks, writings, information, trade secrets, inventions, discoveries, or improvements, whether or not registrable or patentable, which are conceived, constructed, or written by Consultant and arise out of or are related to work and services performed under this agreement, are, or shall become and remain the sole and exclusive property of Contractor, whether or not such intellectual property is conceived during the time such work and services are performed or billed.

9A. **Protection of Intellectual Property:** Contractor and Consultant recognize that under U.S. patent laws, all patent applications must be filed in the name of the true and actual inventor(s) of the subject matter sought to be patented. Thus if Consultant makes any patentable inventions relating to the above project, Consultant agrees to be named as an applicant in any U.S. patent application(s) filed on such invention(s). Actual ownership of such patent applications shall be governed by clause 8.

9B. Consultant shall promptly disclose to Contractor in writing all information pertaining to any intellectual property generated or conceived by Consultant under this Agreement. Consultant hereby assigns and agrees to assign all of Consultant's rights to such intellectual property, including patent rights and foreign priority rights. Consultant hereby expressly agrees, without further charge for time, to do all things and sign all documents deemed by Contractor to be necessary or appropriate to invest in intellectual property, including obtaining for and vesting in Contractor all U.S. and foreign patents and patent applications which Contractor desires to obtain to cover such intellectual property, provided that Contractor shall bear all expenses relating thereto. All reasonable local travel time and expenses shall be borne by Consultant.

10. **Trade Secrets:** Consultant recognizes that all information relating to the above Project disclosed to Consultant by Contractor, and all information generated by Consultant in the performance of the above Work, is a valuable trade secret of Contractor and Consultant shall treat all such information as strictly confidential, during and after the performance of Work under this Agreement. Specifically Consultant shall not reveal, publish, or communicate any such information to anyone other than Contractor, and shall safeguard all such information from access to anyone other than Contractor, except upon the express written authorization of Contractor. This clause shall not apply to any information which Consultant can document in writing is presently in or enters the public domain from a bona fide source other than Consultant.

11. **Return of Property:** Consultant agrees to return all written materials and objects received from Contractor, to deliver to Contractor all objects and a copy (and all copies and originals if requested by Contractor) of all written materials resulting from or relating to work performed under this Agreement, and not to deliver to any person, organization, or publisher, or cause to be published, any such written material without prior written authorization.

12. **Conflicts of Interest:** Consultant recognizes a fiduciary obligation to Contractor arising out of the work and services performed under this agreement and accordingly will not offer Consultant's service to or perform services for any competitor, potential or actual, of Contractor for the above Project, or perform any other acts which may result in any conflict of interest by Consultant, during and after the term of this Agreement.

13. **Mediation and Arbitration:** If any dispute arises under this Agreement, the parties shall negotiate in good faith to settle such dispute. If the parties cannot resolve such dispute themselves, then either party may submit the dispute to mediation by a mediator approved by both parties. If the parties cannot agree to any mediator, or if either party does not wish to abide by any decision of the mediator, they shall submit the dispute to arbitration by any mutually acceptable arbitrator, or the American Arbitration Association (AAA). If the AAA is selected, the arbitration shall take place under the auspices of the nearest branch of such to both parties. The costs of the arbitration proceeding shall be borne according to the decision of the arbitrator, who may apportion costs equally, or in accordance with any finding or fault or lack of good faith of either party. The arbitrator's award shall be nonappealable and enforceable in any court of competent jurisdiction.

14. **Governing Law:** This Agreement shall be governed by and interpreted under and according to the laws of the State of _____.

15. **Signatures:** The parties have indicated their agreement to all of the above terms by signing this Agreement on the respective dates below indicated. Each party has received an original signed copy hereof.

Contractor: _____ Date: _____

Consultant: _____ Date: _____

Proprietary Materials Agreement
(Keep Confidential/Non-Disclosure Agreement)

PROPRIETARY MATERIALS (items, documents, or models loaned—describe or identify fully, including number of sheets):

_____

_____

_____

_____

PROPRIETARY MATERIALS loaned by (name and address):

_____

_____

_____ ("LENDER")

PROPRIETARY MATERIALS loaned to (name and address):

_____

_____

_____ ("BORROWER")

BORROWER acknowledges and agrees as follows:

(1) BORROWER:

[BORROWER cross out (a) and initial (b), or vice versa, as appropriate]

(a) has received the above Proprietary Materials from LENDER (_____)

(b) understands that LENDER will immediately send the above PROPRIETARY MATERIALS to BORROWER upon LENDER'S receipt, from BORROWER, of a signed copy of this Agreement (_____)

(2) These PROPRIETARY MATERIALS contain valuable proprietary information of LENDER. This proprietary information constitutes a trade secret of LENDER and loss or outside disclosure of these materials or the information contained within these materials will harm LENDER economically.

(3) BORROWER acknowledges that these PROPRIETARY MATERIALS are furnished to BORROWER under the following conditions:

(a) These PROPRIETARY MATERIALS and the information they contain shall be used by BORROWER solely to review or evaluate a proposal or information from, supply a quotation to, or provide a component or item for LENDER.

(b) BORROWER agrees not to disclose these PROPRIETARY MATERIALS or the information they contain except to any persons within BORROWER'S organization having a good faith "need to know" same for the purpose of fulfilling the terms of this Agreement. If necessary, BORROWER may make additional copies of this Agreement and have each such person sign a copy of this Agreement and furnish such copy(ies) to LENDER.

(c) BORROWER and all persons within BORROWER'S organization shall exercise a high degree of care to safeguard these PROPRIETARY MATERIALS and the information they contain from access or disclosure to all unauthorized persons.

(d) BORROWER shall not make any copies of these PROPRIETARY MATERIALS except upon written permission of LENDER and BORROWER shall return all PROPRIETARY MATERIALS (including any copies made) to LENDER at any time upon request by LENDER.

(4) These terms shall not apply to any information which BORROWER can document becomes part of the general public knowledge without fault of BORROWER or comes into BORROWER'S possession in good faith without restriction.

BORROWER: _____

(Name of Organization or Individual)

By: _____

_____

(Name and Title)

Date: _____ / _____ / _____

Other persons within BORROWER'S organization obtaining access to PROPRIETARY MATERIALS:

_____ _____ / _____ / _____

Print Name: _____

_____ _____ / _____ / _____

Print Name: _____

Proprietary Materials Agreement

(Keep Confidential/Non-Disclosure Agreement)

PROPRIETARY MATERIALS (items, documents, or models loaned—describe or identify fully, including number of sheets):

_____

_____

_____

_____

PROPRIETARY MATERIALS loaned by (name and address):

_____

_____

_____ ("LENDER")

PROPRIETARY MATERIALS loaned to (name and address):

_____

_____

_____ ("BORROWER")

BORROWER acknowledges and agrees as follows:

(1) BORROWER:

    [BORROWER cross out (a) and initial (b), or vice versa, as appropriate]

    (a) has received the above Proprietary Materials from LENDER (_____)

    (b) understands that LENDER will immediately send the above PROPRIETARY MATERIALS to BORROWER upon LENDER'S receipt, from BORROWER, of a signed copy of this Agreement (_____)

(2) These PROPRIETARY MATERIALS contain valuable proprietary information of LENDER. This proprietary information constitutes a trade secret of LENDER and loss or outside disclosure of these materials or the information contained within these materials will harm LENDER economically.

(3) BORROWER acknowledges that these PROPRIETARY MATERIALS are furnished to BORROWER under the following conditions:

    (a) These PROPRIETARY MATERIALS and the information they contain shall be used by BORROWER solely to review or evaluate a proposal or information from, supply a quotation to, or provide a component or item for LENDER.

    (b) BORROWER agrees not to disclose these PROPRIETARY MATERIALS or the information they contain except to any persons within BORROWER'S organization having a good faith "need to know" same for the purpose of fulfilling the terms of this Agreement. If necessary, BORROWER may make additional copies of this Agreement and have each such person sign a copy of this Agreement and furnish such copy(ies) to LENDER.

    (c) BORROWER and all persons within BORROWER'S organization shall exercise a high degree of care to safeguard these PROPRIETARY MATERIALS and the information they contain from access or disclosure to all unauthorized persons.

(d) BORROWER shall not make any copies of these PROPRIETARY MATERIALS except upon written permission of LENDER and BORROWER shall return all PROPRIETARY MATERIALS (including any copies made) to LENDER at any time upon request by LENDER.

(4) These terms shall not apply to any information which BORROWER can document becomes part of the general public knowledge without fault of BORROWER or comes into BORROWER'S possession in good faith without restriction.

BORROWER: _____

(Name of Organization or Individual)

By: _____

_____

(Name and Title)

Date: _____ / _____ / _____

Other persons within BORROWER'S organization obtaining access to PROPRIETARY MATERIALS:

_____ _____ / _____ / _____

Print Name: _____

_____ _____ / _____ / _____

Print Name: _____

Proprietary Materials Agreement

(Keep Confidential/Non-Disclosure Agreement)

PROPRIETARY MATERIALS (items, documents, or models loaned—describe or identify fully, including number of sheets):

_____

_____

_____

_____

PROPRIETARY MATERIALS loaned by (name and address):

_____

_____

_____ ("LENDER")

PROPRIETARY MATERIALS loaned to (name and address):

_____

_____

_____ ("BORROWER")

BORROWER acknowledges and agrees as follows:

(1) BORROWER:

    [BORROWER cross out (a) and initial (b), or vice versa, as appropriate]

    (a) has received the above Proprietary Materials from LENDER (_____)

    (b) understands that LENDER will immediately send the above PROPRIETARY MATERIALS to BORROWER upon LENDER'S receipt, from BORROWER, of a signed copy of this Agreement (_____)

(2) These PROPRIETARY MATERIALS contain valuable proprietary information of LENDER. This proprietary information constitutes a trade secret of LENDER and loss or outside disclosure of these materials or the information contained within these materials will harm LENDER economically.

(3) BORROWER acknowledges that these PROPRIETARY MATERIALS are furnished to BORROWER under the following conditions:

    (a) These PROPRIETARY MATERIALS and the information they contain shall be used by BORROWER solely to review or evaluate a proposal or information from, supply a quotation to, or provide a component or item for LENDER.

    (b) BORROWER agrees not to disclose these PROPRIETARY MATERIALS or the information they contain except to any persons within BORROWER'S organization having a good faith "need to know" same for the purpose of fulfilling the terms of this Agreement. If necessary, BORROWER may make additional copies of this Agreement and have each such person sign a copy of this Agreement and furnish such copy(ies) to LENDER.

    (c) BORROWER and all persons within BORROWER'S organization shall exercise a high degree of care to safeguard these PROPRIETARY MATERIALS and the information they contain from access or disclosure to all unauthorized persons.

(d) BORROWER shall not make any copies of these PROPRIETARY MATERIALS except upon written permission of LENDER and BORROWER shall return all PROPRIETARY MATERIALS (including any copies made) to LENDER at any time upon request by LENDER.

(4) These terms shall not apply to any information which BORROWER can document becomes part of the general public knowledge without fault of BORROWER or comes into BORROWER'S possession in good faith without restriction.

BORROWER: _____

(Name of Organization or Individual)

By: _____

_____

(Name and Title)

Date: _____ / _____ / _____

Other persons within BORROWER'S organization obtaining access to PROPRIETARY MATERIALS:

_____   _____ / _____ / _____

Print Name: _____

_____   _____ / _____ / _____

Print Name: _____

Proprietary Materials Agreement

(Keep Confidential/Non-Disclosure Agreement)

PROPRIETARY MATERIALS (items, documents, or models loaned—describe or identify fully, including number of sheets):

_____

_____

_____

_____

PROPRIETARY MATERIALS loaned by (name and address):

_____

_____

_____ ("LENDER")

PROPRIETARY MATERIALS loaned to (name and address):

_____

_____

_____ ("BORROWER")

BORROWER acknowledges and agrees as follows:

(1) BORROWER:

[BORROWER cross out (a) and initial (b), or vice versa, as appropriate]

(a) has received the above Proprietary Materials from LENDER (_____)

(b) understands that LENDER will immediately send the above PROPRIETARY MATERIALS to BORROWER upon LENDER'S receipt, from BORROWER, of a signed copy of this Agreement (_____)

(2) These PROPRIETARY MATERIALS contain valuable proprietary information of LENDER. This proprietary information constitutes a trade secret of LENDER and loss or outside disclosure of these materials or the information contained within these materials will harm LENDER economically.

(3) BORROWER acknowledges that these PROPRIETARY MATERIALS are furnished to BORROWER under the following conditions:

(a) These PROPRIETARY MATERIALS and the information they contain shall be used by BORROWER solely to review or evaluate a proposal or information from, supply a quotation to, or provide a component or item for LENDER.

(b) BORROWER agrees not to disclose these PROPRIETARY MATERIALS or the information they contain except to any persons within BORROWER'S organization having a good faith "need to know" same for the purpose of fulfilling the terms of this Agreement. If necessary, BORROWER may make additional copies of this Agreement and have each such person sign a copy of this Agreement and furnish such copy(ies) to LENDER.

(c) BORROWER and all persons within BORROWER'S organization shall exercise a high degree of care to safeguard these PROPRIETARY MATERIALS and the information they contain from access or disclosure to all unauthorized persons.

(d) BORROWER shall not make any copies of these PROPRIETARY MATERIALS except upon written permission of LENDER and BORROWER shall return all PROPRIETARY MATERIALS (including any copies made) to LENDER at any time upon request by LENDER.

(4) These terms shall not apply to any information which BORROWER can document becomes part of the general public knowledge without fault of BORROWER or comes into BORROWER'S possession in good faith without restriction.

BORROWER:_____

(Name of Organization or Individual)

By: _____

_____

(Name and Title)

Date: _____ /_____ /_____

Other persons within BORROWER'S organization obtaining access to PROPRIETARY MATERIALS:

_____ _____ /_____ /_____

Print Name: _____

_____ _____ /_____ /_____

Print Name: _____

Proprietary Materials Agreement
(Keep Confidential/Non-Disclosure Agreement)

PROPRIETARY MATERIALS (items, documents, or models loaned—describe or identify fully, including number of sheets):

_____

_____

_____

_____

PROPRIETARY MATERIALS loaned by (name and address):

_____

_____

_____ ("LENDER")

PROPRIETARY MATERIALS loaned to (name and address):

_____

_____

_____ ("BORROWER")

BORROWER acknowledges and agrees as follows:

(1) BORROWER:

   [BORROWER cross out (a) and initial (b), or vice versa, as appropriate]

   (a) has received the above Proprietary Materials from LENDER (_____)

   (b) understands that LENDER will immediately send the above PROPRIETARY MATERIALS to BORROWER upon LENDER'S receipt, from BORROWER, of a signed copy of this Agreement (_____)

(2) These PROPRIETARY MATERIALS contain valuable proprietary information of LENDER. This proprietary information constitutes a trade secret of LENDER and loss or outside disclosure of these materials or the information contained within these materials will harm LENDER economically.

(3) BORROWER acknowledges that these PROPRIETARY MATERIALS are furnished to BORROWER under the following conditions:

   (a) These PROPRIETARY MATERIALS and the information they contain shall be used by BORROWER solely to review or evaluate a proposal or information from, supply a quotation to, or provide a component or item for LENDER.

   (b) BORROWER agrees not to disclose these PROPRIETARY MATERIALS or the information they contain except to any persons within BORROWER'S organization having a good faith "need to know" same for the purpose of fulfilling the terms of this Agreement. If necessary, BORROWER may make additional copies of this Agreement and have each such person sign a copy of this Agreement and furnish such copy(ies) to LENDER.

   (c) BORROWER and all persons within BORROWER'S organization shall exercise a high degree of care to safeguard these PROPRIETARY MATERIALS and the information they contain from access or disclosure to all unauthorized persons.

(d) BORROWER shall not make any copies of these PROPRIETARY MATERIALS except upon written permission of LENDER and BORROWER shall return all PROPRIETARY MATERIALS (including any copies made) to LENDER at any time upon request by LENDER.

(4) These terms shall not apply to any information which BORROWER can document becomes part of the general public knowledge without fault of BORROWER or comes into BORROWER'S possession in good faith without restriction.

BORROWER: _____

(Name of Organization or Individual)

By: _____

_____

(Name and Title)

Date: _____ / _____ / _____

Other persons within BORROWER'S organization obtaining access to PROPRIETARY MATERIALS:

_____ _____ / _____ / _____

Print Name: _____

_____ _____ / _____ / _____

Print Name: _____

Joint Owners' Agreement

This agreement is made by and between the following parties who, by separate assignment or as joint applicants, own the following respective shares of the invention, patent application or patent identified below:

_____ of _____ , _____%,

_____ of _____ , _____%,

_____ of _____ , _____%,

Invention Title: _____

Patent Application Ser. Nr.: _____ , Filed: _____

Patent Nr.: _____ , Issued: _____

Applicants: _____

The above patent application data is to be filled in as soon as it becomes available if the application has not yet been filed.

The parties desire to stipulate the terms under which they will exploit this invention and patent application and therefore agree as follows:

1. **No Action Without Everyone's Consent:** None of the parties to this agreement shall license, use, make, or sell the invention or application, or take any other action, other than normal prosecution, without the written consent and cooperation of the other party or parties (hereinafter "parties") to this agreement, except as provided below. Any action so taken shall be committed to a writing signed by all of the parties, or as many parties as consent, with copies to all other parties.

2. **Decisions:** In case any decision must be made in connection with the invention or the patent application, including foreign filing, appealing from an adverse decision in the Patent and Trademark Office, or any opportunity to license, sell, make, or use the invention or application, the parties shall consult on such opportunity and a majority decision shall control. In the event the parties are equally divided, the matter shall be decided in accordance with Paragraph 5 below. After a decision is so made, all parties shall abide by the decision and shall cooperate fully by whatever means are necessary to implement and give full force to such decision. However, if an offer is involved and there is time for any parties to obtain a better or different offer, they shall be entitled to do so and the decision shall be postponed for up to one month to allow such other parties to act.

3. **Proportionate Sharing:** The parties to this agreement shall share, in the percentages indicated above, in all income from, liabilities, and expenditures agreed to be made by any decision under Part 2 above in connection with the invention or patent application. In case a decision is made to make any expenditure, as for foreign patent application filing, exploitation, etc., and a minority or other parties opposes such expenditure or is unable to contribute his or her proportionate share, then the others shall advance the minority or other parties' share of the expenditure. Such others shall be reimbursed by the minority or other parties by double the amount so advanced from the minority or other parties' proportionate share of any income received, provided such income has some reasonable connection with the expenditure. No party shall be

entitled to reimbursement or credit for any labor unless agreed to in advance by all of the parties hereto.

4. **If Any Parties Desire to Manufacture, Etc.:** If any parties who do not constitute all of the parties to this agreement desire to manufacture, distribute, or sell any product or service embodying the above invention, they may do so with the written consent of the other parties under Part 1 above. The cost of the product or service shall include, in addition to normal profit, labor, commission, and/or overhead, etc., provision for a reasonable royalty which shall be paid for the term of the above patent application and any patent which may issue thereon. Such royalty shall be determined before any action is taken under this part and as if a valid patent on the invention had been licensed to an unrelated exclusive licensee (or a nonexclusive licensee if the patent is licensed to others) in an arm's length transaction. Such royalty shall be distributed to all of the parties hereto according to their proportionate shares and on a quarterly basis, accompanied by a written royalty report and sent within one month after the close of each calendar quarter.

5. **In Case of Dispute:** In case any dispute, disagreement, or need for any decision arises out of this agreement or in connection with the invention or patent application, and the parties cannot settle the matter or come to a decision in accordance with Paragraph 2, above, the parties shall first confer as much as necessary to settle the disagreement; all parties shall act and compromise to at least the degree a reasonable person would act. If the parties cannot settle their differences or come to a decision on their own, they shall submit the dispute or matter to mediation and decision by an impartial third party or professional mediator agreed to by all of the parties. If the parties cannot agree on a mediator, or cannot come to an agreement after mediation, then they shall submit the matter to binding arbitration with a mutually acceptable arbitrator or the American Arbitration Association. The arbitrator shall settle the dispute in whatever manner he or she feels will do substantial justice, recognizing the rights of all parties and commercial realities of the marketplace. The parties shall abide by the terms of the arbitrator's decision and shall cooperate fully and do any acts necessary to implement such decision. The costs of the arbitrator shall be advanced by all of the parties or in accordance with Part 3 above and the arbitrator may make any allocation of arbitration costs he or she feels is reasonable.

6. **Non-Frustration:** Neither party to this Agreement shall commit any act or take any action which frustrates or hampers the rights of the other party under this Agreement. Each party shall act in good faith and engage in fair dealing when taking any action under or related to this Agreement.

_____ Signature	_____ Date
_____ Signature	_____ Date
_____ Signature	_____ Date

Assignment of Invention and Patent Application

For value received,_____,

_____

of _____

_____

(hereinafter Assignor), hereby sells, assigns, transfers, and sets over unto _____

_____

of _____

and her or his successors or assigns (hereinafter Assignee) _____% of the following: (A) ASSIGNOR'S

right, title and interest in and to the invention entitled " _____

_____ "

invented by Assignor; (B) the application for United States patent therefor, signed by Assignor on

_____ , U.S. Patent and Trademark Office Serial Number _____,

filed _____; (C) any patent or reissues of any patent that may be granted

thereon; and (D) any applications which are continuations, continuations-in-part, substitutes, or

divisions of said application. Assignor authorizes Assignee to enter the date of signature and/or

Serial Number and Filing Date in the spaces above. Assignor also authorizes and requests the

Assistant Commissioner for Patents to issue any resulting patent(s) as follows: _____% to Assignor

and _____% to Assignee. (The singular shall include the plural and vice versa herein.)

ASSIGNOR hereby further sells, assigns, transfers, and sets over unto ASSIGNEE, the above
percentage of ASSIGNOR'S entire right, title and interest in and to said invention in each and every
country foreign to the United States; and ASSIGNOR further conveys to ASSIGNEE the above
percentage of all priority rights resulting from the above-identified application for United States
patent. ASSIGNOR agrees to execute all papers, give any required testimony and perform other
lawful acts, at ASSIGNEE'S expense, as ASSIGNEE may require to enable ASSIGNEE to perfect
ASSIGNEE'S interest in any resulting patent of the United States and countries foreign thereto, and
to acquire, hold, enforce, convey, and uphold the validity of said patent and reissues and extensions
thereof, and ASSIGNEE'S interest therein.

In testimony whereof ASSIGNOR has hereunto set its hand and seal on the date below.

_____

_____

State: _____
County: _____ } ss

Subscribed and sworn to before me _____, _____.

_____
Notary Public

SEAL

Universal License Agreement

1. **Parties and Summary of Terms:**

    Parties: This agreement is between:

    Licensor: _____ ,

    of _____ .

    Licensee: _____ ,

    of _____ .

    Summary: Type of License: ☐ Exclusive ☐ Nonexclusive

    Invention Title: _____ .

    Patent Application Ser. Nr.: _____ , Filing Date: _____

    If Exclusive License, minimum number of units to be sold to compute Minimum Annual Royalty (MAR): _____

      MARs start first quarter of _____ .

    ☐ Option Granted: Premium $ _____ For term of: _____ (months)

    Patent Royalty Rate _____ % ☐ Know-How Licensed: Know-How Royalty Rate: _____ %

    Total Royalty Rate (Patent Royalty Rate plus Know-How Royalty, if applicable): _____ %.

    Estimated 1st year's sales (units): _____ x Estimated Unit Price $ _____

      x Total Royalty Rate _____ % = Licensing Fee $ _____

2. **Effective Date:** This agreement shall be effective as of the later of the signature dates below written and shall be referred to as the Agreement of such date.

3. **Recitals:**

    A. **LICENSOR** has developed an invention having the above title and warrants that LICENSOR has filed a patent application on such invention in the U.S. Patent and Trademark Office, which patent application is identified by the above title, Serial Number, and Filing Date. LICENSOR warrants that LICENSOR has full and exclusive right to grant this license on this invention and LICENSOR'S patent application. If the "Know-How Licensed" box above is checked, LICENSOR has also developed know-how in connection with said invention and warrants that LICENSOR owns and has the right to license said know-how.

    B. **LICENSEE** desires, if the "Option Granted" box above is checked, to exclusively investigate LICENSOR'S above invention for the term indicated. If said "Option Granted" box is not checked, or if said box is checked and LICENSEE investigates LICENSOR'S invention for the term indicated and such investigation is favorable, LICENSEE desires to make, use and sell the products embodying such invention and covered by the claims of LICENSOR'S patent application and any patent(s) issuing thereon (hereinafter "Licensed Product").

4. **If Option Granted:** If the "Option Granted" box above is checked, then (A) the patent license grant of Part 5 below shall not take effect except as defined in this part, and (B) LICENSOR hereby grants LICENSEE, for the option premium stated above, an exclusive option to investigate LICENSOR'S invention for the term indicated above, such term to commence from the date of this Agreement. LICENSOR will furnish LICENSEE with all information and know-how (if any) concerning LICENSOR'S invention in LICENSOR'S possession. LICENSEE will investigate LICENSOR'S invention for operability, costing, marketing, etc. LICENSEE shall report the results of its investigation to LICENSOR at any time before the end of the option term. If LICENSEE'S determination is favorable, it may thereupon exercise this option and the patent license grant of Part 5 below shall become effective. If LICENSEE'S determination is unfavorable, then said option shall not be exercised and no patent license grant shall take effect, all rights hereunder shall revert to LICENSOR, LICENSEE shall deliver to LICENSOR all

results of its investigations for LICENSOR'S benefit, and LICENSEE shall promptly return to LICENSOR all know-how (papers and things) received from LICENSOR or generated by LICENSEE in its investigations.

5. **Patent License If Option Exercised or If Option Not Granted:** If the "Option Granted" box above is checked and LICENSEE has investigated LICENSOR'S invention and such investigation is favorable and LICENSEE has exercised its option, or if said box is not checked, then LICENSOR hereby grants to LICENSEE, subject to the terms and conditions herein, a patent license of the type (Exclusive or Nonexclusive) checked above. Such patent license shall include the right to grant sublicenses, to make, have made, use, and sell the Licensed Product throughout the United States, its territories, and possessions. Such patent license shall be under LICENSOR'S patent application, any continuations, divisions, continuations-in-part, substitutes, reissues of any patent from any of such applications (hereinafter and hereinbefore LICENSOR'S patent application), any patent(s) issuing thereon, and if the "Know-How Licensed" box is checked above, any know-how transferred to LICENSEE.

6. **If Know-How Licensed:** If the "Know-How" box above is checked, LICENSOR shall communicate to LICENSEE all of LICENSOR'S know-how in respect of LICENSOR'S invention within one month after the date of this Agreement and shall be available to consult with LICENSEE, for up to 80 hours, with respect to the licensed invention and know-how. All travel and other expenses of LICENSOR for such consultation shall be reimbursed by LICENSEE within one month after LICENSOR submits its voucher therefor. LICENSOR makes no warranty regarding the value, suitability, or workability of such know-how. The royalty applicable for such know-how shall be paid, at the rate indicated above, for a minimum of three years from the date of this Agreement if no option is granted, or for three years from the date of exercise if an option is granted and exercised by LICENSOR, and thereafter for so long as LICENSEE makes, uses, or sells Licensed Products and has a share in the United States of at least 15% of the competitive market for Licensed Products.

7. **Royalties:**

   A. **Licensing Fee:** Unless the "Option Granted" box above is checked, LICENSEE shall pay to LICENSOR, upon execution of this Agreement, a nonrefundable Licensing Fee. This Licensing Fee shall also serve as an advance against future royalties. Such Licensing Fee shall be computed as follows: (A) Take the Total Royalty Rate in percent, as stated above. (B) Multiply by LICENSEE'S Estimate of Its First Year's Sales, in units of Licensed Product, as stated above. (C) Multiply by LICENSEE'S Estimated Unit Price of Licensed Product, in dollars, as stated above. (D) The combined product shall be the Licensing Fee, in dollars, as stated above. When LICENSEE begins actual sales of the Licensed Product, it shall certify its Actual Net Factory Sales Price of Licensed Product to LICENSOR in writing and shall either (1) simultaneously pay LICENSOR any difference due if the Actual Net Factory Sales Price of Licensed Product is more than the Estimated Unit Price, stated above, or (2) advise LICENSOR of any credit to which LICENSEE is entitled if the Actual Net Factory Sales Price of Licensed Product is less than the above Estimated Unit Price. In the latter case, LICENSEE may deduct such credit from its first royalty remittance to LICENSOR, under subpart B below. If an option is granted and exercised under Part 4 above, then LICENSEE shall pay this Licensing Fee to LICENSOR if and when LICENSEE exercises its option.

   B. **Royalty:** If the "Option Granted" box above is not checked, or if said box is checked and LICENSEE has exercised its option under Part 4, LICENSEE shall also pay to LICENSOR a Total Royalty, at the rate stated above. Such royalty shall be at the Patent Royalty Rate stated in Part 1 above, plus, if the "Know-How Licensed" box above is checked, a Know-

How Royalty at the Know-How Royalty Rate stated above. Said Total Royalty shall be computed on LICENSEE'S Net Factory Sales Price of Licensed Product. Such Total Royalty shall accrue when the Licensed Products are first sold or disposed of by LICENSEE, or by any sublicensee of LICENSEE. LICENSEE shall pay the Total Royalty due to LICENSOR within one month after the end of each calendar quarter, together with a written report to LICENSOR of the number of units, respective sales prices, and total sales made in such quarter, together with a full itemization of any adjustments made pursuant to subpart F below. LICENSEE'S first report and payment shall be made within one month after the end of the first calendar quarter following the execution of this Agreement. No royalties shall be paid by LICENSEE to LICENSOR until after the Licensing Fee under subpart A above has been earned, but LICENSEE shall make a quarterly report hereunder for every calendar quarter after the execution hereof, whether or not any royalty payment is due for such quarter, except that if an option is granted, LICENSEE shall not make any royalty reports until and if LICENSEE exercises its option.

C. **Minimum Annual Royalties:** If the "Exclusive" box above is checked, so that this is an exclusive license, then this subpart C and subpart D shall be applicable. But if the "Nonexclusive" box is checked above, then these subparts C and D shall be inapplicable. There shall be no minimum annual royalties due under this Agreement until the "Year Commencing," as identified in Part 1 above. For the exclusivity privilege of the patent license grant under Part 5 above, a Minimum Annual Royalty shall be due beginning with such royalty year and for each royalty year ending on the anniversary of such royalty year thereafter. Such Minimum Annual Royalty shall be equal to the Patent Royalty which would have been due if the "Minimum Number of Units [of Licensed Product] to Be Sold to Compute Minimum Annual Royalty" identified in Part 1 above were sold during such royalty year. If less than such number of units of Licensed Product are sold in any royalty year, then the Patent Royalty payable for the fourth quarter of such year shall be increased so as to cause the Patent Royalties paid for such year to equal said Minimum Annual Royalty. If an option is granted under Parts 1 and 4, then no Minimum Annual Royalties shall be due in any case until and if LICENSEE exercises its option.

D. **If Minimum Not Paid:** If this part is applicable and if sales of Licensed Product in any royalty year do not equal or exceed the minimum number of units identified in Part 1 above, LICENSEE may choose not to pay the Minimum Annual Royalty under subpart C above. In this case, LICENSEE shall so notify LICENSOR by the date on which the last royalty for such year is due, i.e., within one month after any anniversary of the date identified in Part 1 above. Thereupon the license grant under Part 4 above shall be converted to a nonexclusive grant, and LICENSOR may immediately license others under the above patent.

E. **Most Favored Licensee:** If this license is nonexclusive, or if it becomes nonexclusive under subpart D above, then (a) LICENSOR shall not grant any other license under the above patent to any other party under any terms which are more favorable than those which LICENSEE pays or enjoys under this Agreement, and (b) LICENSOR shall promptly advise LICENSEE of any such other grant and the terms thereof.

F. **When No Royalties Due:** No Patent Royalties shall be due under this Agreement after the above patent expires or if it is declared invalid by a court of competent jurisdiction from which no appeal can be taken. Also, if LICENSOR'S patent application becomes finally abandoned without any patent issuing, then the Patent Royalty under this Agreement shall be terminated as of the date of abandonment. Any Know-How Royalties under Part 6 above shall continue after any Patent Royalties terminate, provided such Know-How Royalties are otherwise due under such Part 6.

G. **Late Payments:** If any payment due under this Agreement is not timely paid, then the unpaid balance shall bear interest until paid at an annual rate of 10% until the delinquent balance is paid. Such interest shall be compounded monthly.

H. **Net Factory Sales Price:** "Net Factory Sales Price" is defined as the gross factory selling price of Licensed Product, or the U.S. importer's gross selling price if Licensed Product is made abroad, less usual trade discounts actually allowed, but not including advertising allowances or fees or commissions paid to employees or agents of LICENSEE. The Net Factory Sales Price shall not include (1) packing costs, if itemized separately, (2) import and export taxes, excise and other sales taxes, and customs duties, and (3) costs of insurance and transportation, if separately billed, from the place of manufacture if in the U.S., or from the place of importation if manufactured abroad, to the customer's premises or next point of distribution or sale. Bona fide returns may be deducted from units shipped in computing the royalty payable after such returns are made.

8. **Records:** LICENSEE and any of its sublicensees shall keep full, clear, and accurate records with respect to sales subject to royalty under this Agreement. The records shall be made in a manner such that the royalty reports made pursuant to Part 7B can be verified. LICENSOR, or its authorized agent, shall have the right to examine and audit such records upon reasonable notice during normal business hours, but not more than twice per year. In case of any dispute as to the sufficiency or accuracy of such records, LICENSOR may have any independent auditor examine and certify such records. LICENSEE shall make prompt adjustment to compensate for any errors or omissions disclosed by any such examination and certification of LICENSEE'S records. If LICENSOR does not examine LICENSEE'S records or question any royalty report within two years from the date thereof, then such report shall be considered final and LICENSOR shall have no further right to contest such report.

9. **Sublicensees:** If LICENSEE grants any sublicenses hereunder, it shall notify LICENSOR within one month from any such grant and shall provide LICENSOR with a true copy of any sublicense agreement. Any sublicensee of LICENSEE under this Agreement shall be bound by all of the terms applying to LICENSEE hereunder and LICENSEE shall be responsible for the obligations and duties of any of its sublicensees.

10. **Patent Prosecution:**

A. **Domestic:** LICENSOR shall, at LICENSOR'S own expense, prosecute its above U.S. patent application, and any continuations, divisions, continuations-in-part, substitutes, and reissues of such patent application or any patent thereon, at its own expense, until all applicable patents issue or any patent application becomes finally abandoned. LICENSOR shall also pay any maintenance fees which are due on any patent(s) which issue on said patent application. If for any reason LICENSOR intends to abandon any patent application hereunder, it shall notify LICENSEE at least two months in advance of any such abandonment so as to give LICENSEE the opportunity to take over prosecution of any such application and maintenance of any patent. If LICENSEE takes over prosecution, LICENSOR shall cooperate with LICENSEE in any manner LICENSEE requires, at LICENSEE'S expense.

B. **Foreign:** LICENSOR shall have the opportunity, but not the obligation, to file corresponding foreign patent applications to any patent application under subpart A above. If LICENSOR files any such foreign patent applications, LICENSOR may license, sell, or otherwise exploit the invention, Licensed Product, or any such foreign application in any countries foreign to the United States as it chooses, provided that LICENSOR must give LICENSEE a right of first refusal and at least one month to exercise this right before undertaking any such foreign exploitation. If LICENSOR chooses not to file any corresponding foreign applications under this part, it shall notify LICENSEE at least one month prior to the first anniversary of the above patent application so as to give LICENSEE the opportunity to file corresponding foreign patent applications if it so chooses.

    C. If Licensee Acts: If LICENSEE takes over prosecution of any U.S. patent application under subpart A above, and LICENSEE is successful so that a patent issues, then LICENSEE shall pay LICENSOR royalties thereafter at a rate of 75% of the royalty rate and any applicable minimum under Part 7C above and LICENSEE shall be entitled to deduct prosecution and maintenance expenses from its royalty payments. If LICENSEE elects to prosecute any foreign patent applications under subpart B above, then LICENSEE shall pay LICENSOR royalties of 50% of the royalty rate under Part 7 above for any applicable foreign sales, less all foreign prosecution and maintenance expenses incurred by LICENSEE.

11. **Marking:** LICENSEE shall mark all units of Licensed Product, or its container if direct marking is not feasible, with the legend "Patent Pending" until any patent(s) issue from the above patent application. When any patent(s) issue, LICENSOR shall promptly notify LICENSEE and thereafter LICENSEE shall mark all units of Licensed Product which it sells with proper notice of patent marking under 35 U.S.C. Section 287.

12. **If Infringement Occurs:** If either party discovers that the above patent is infringed, it shall communicate the details to the other party. LICENSOR shall thereupon have the right, but not the obligation, to take whatever action it deems necessary, including the filing of lawsuits, to protect the rights of the parties to this Agreement and to terminate such infringement. LICENSEE shall cooperate with LICENSOR if LICENSOR takes any such action, but all expenses of LICENSOR shall be borne by LICENSOR. If LICENSOR recovers any damages or compensation for any action it takes hereunder, LICENSOR shall retain 100% of such damages. If LICENSOR does not wish to take any action hereunder, LICENSEE shall also have the right, but not the obligation, to take any such action, in which case LICENSOR shall cooperate with LICENSEE, but all of LICENSEE'S expenses shall be borne by LICENSEE. LICENSEE shall receive 75% of any damages or compensation it recovers for any such infringement and shall pay 25% of such damages or compensation to LICENSOR, after deducting its costs, including attorney fees.

13. **Disclaimer and Hold Harmless:**

    A. Disclaimer of Warranty: Nothing herein shall be construed as a warranty or representation by LICENSOR as to the scope or validity of the above patent application or any patent issuing thereon.

    B. Product Liability: LICENSEE shall hold LICENSOR harmless from any product liability actions involving Licensed Product.

14. **Term:** The term of this Agreement shall end with the expiration of the last of any patent(s) which issues on LICENSOR'S patent application, unless terminated sooner for any reason provided herein, or unless know-how is licensed, in which case the terms of Part 6 shall cover the term of this Agreement.

15. **Termination:** This Agreement may be terminated under and according to any of the following contingencies:

    A. Default: If LICENSEE fails to make any payment on the date such payment is due under this Agreement, or if LICENSEE makes any other default under or breach of this Agreement, LICENSOR shall have the right to terminate this Agreement upon giving three months' written Notice of Intent to Terminate, specifying such failure, breach, or default to

LICENSEE. If LICENSEE fails to make any payment in arrears, or otherwise fails to cure the breach or default within such three-month period, then LICENSOR may then send a written Notice of Termination to LICENSEE, whereupon this Agreement shall terminate in one month from the date of such Notice of Termination. If this Agreement is terminated hereunder, LICENSEE shall not be relieved of any of its obligations to the date of termination and LICENSOR may act to enforce LICENSEE'S obligations after any such termination.

B. **Bankruptcy, Etc.:** If LICENSEE shall go into receivership, bankruptcy, or insolvency, or make an assignment for the benefit of creditors, or go out of business, this Agreement shall be immediately terminable by LICENSOR by written notice, but without prejudice to any rights of LICENSOR hereunder.

C. **Antishelving:** If LICENSEE discontinues its sales or manufacture of Licensed Product without intent to resume, it shall so notify LICENSOR within one month of such discontinuance, whereupon LICENSOR shall have the right to terminate this Agreement upon one month's written notice, even if this Agreement has been converted to a nonexclusive grant under Part 7D above. If LICENSEE does not begin manufacture or sales of Licensed Product within one and one-half years from the date of this Agreement or the date of its option exercise if an option is granted, or, after commencing manufacture and sales of Licensed Product, discontinues its manufacture and sales of Licensed Product for one and one-half years, LICENSOR shall have the right to terminate this Agreement upon one months' written notice, unless LICENSEE can show that it in good faith intends and is actually working to resume or begin manufacture or sales, and has a reasonable basis to justify its delay. In such case LICENSEE shall advise LICENSOR in writing, before the end of such one-and-one-half-year period, of the circumstances involved and LICENSEE shall thereupon have up to an additional year to resume or begin manufacture or sales. It is the intent of the parties hereto that LICENSOR shall not be deprived of the opportunity, for an unreasonable length of time, to exclusively license its patent if LICENSEE has discontinued or has not commenced manufacture or sales of Licensed Product. In no case shall LICENSOR have the right to terminate this Agreement if and so long as LICENSEE is paying LICENSOR minimum annual royalties under Part 7C above.

16. **Notices:** All notices, payments, or statements under this Agreement shall be in writing and shall be sent by first-class certified mail, return receipt requested, postage prepaid, to the party concerned at the above address, or to any substituted address given by notice hereunder. Any such notice, payment, or statement shall be considered sent or made on the day deposited in the mails. Payments and statements may be sent by ordinary mail.

17. **Mediation and Arbitration:** If any dispute arises under this Agreement, the parties shall negotiate in good faith to settle such dispute. If the parties cannot resolve such dispute themselves, then either party may submit the dispute to mediation by a mediator approved by both parties. The parties shall both cooperate with the mediator. If the parties cannot agree to any mediator, or if either party does not wish to abide by any decision of the mediator, then they shall submit the dispute to arbitration by any mutually acceptable arbitrator. If no arbitrator is mutually acceptable, then they shall submit the matter to arbitration under the rules of the American Arbitration Association (AAA). Under any arbitration, both parties shall cooperate with and agree to abide finally by any decision of the arbitration proceeding. If the AAA is selected, the arbitration shall take place under the auspices of the nearest branch of the AAA to the party seeking arbitration. The costs of the arbitration proceeding shall be borne according to the decision of the arbitrator, who may apportion costs equally, or in accordance

with any finding of fault or lack of good faith of either party. The arbitrator's award shall be non-appealable and enforceable in any court of competent jurisdiction.

18. **Assignment:** The rights of LICENSOR under this Agreement shall be assignable or otherwise transferrable, in whole or in part, by LICENSOR and shall vest LICENSOR'S assigns or transferees with the same rights and obligations as were held by LICENSOR. This Agreement shall be assignable by LICENSEE to any entity that succeeds to the business of LICENSEE to which Licensed Products relate or to any other entity if LICENSOR'S permission is first obtained in writing.

19. **Jurisdiction and Venue:** This Agreement shall be interpreted under the laws of LICENSOR'S state, as given in Part 1 above. Any action related to this Agreement shall be brought in the county of LICENSOR'S above address; LICENSEE hereby consents to such venue.

20. **Non-Frustration:** Neither party to this Agreement shall commit any act or take any action which frustrates or hampers the rights of the other party under this Agreement. Each party shall act in good faith and engage in fair dealing when taking any action under or related to this Agreement.

21. **No Challenge:** LICENSEE has investigated the validity of LICENSOR'S patent and shall not challenge, contest, or impugn the validity of such patent.

22. **Rectification:** In case of any mistake in this Agreement, including any error, ambiguity, illegality, contradiction, or omission, this Agreement shall be interpreted as if such mistake were rectified in a manner which implements the intent of the parties as nearly as possible and effects substantial fairness, considering all pertinent circumstances.

23. **Entire Agreement:** This Agreement sets forth the entire understanding between the parties and supersedes any prior or contemporaneous oral understandings and any prior written agreements.

24. **Signatures:** The parties, having carefully read this Agreement and having consulted or have been given an opportunity to consult counsel, have indicated their agreement to all of the above terms by signing this Agreement on the respective dates below indicated. LICENSEE and LICENSOR have each received a copy of this Agreement with both LICENSEE'S and LICENSOR'S original ink signatures thereon.

Licensor: _____   Date: _____

Print Licensor's Name: _____

Licensee: _____   Date: _____

Print Licensee's Name: _____

Request for Participation in Disclosure Document Program

Date: _____

Box DD
Assistant Commissioner for Patents
Washington, District of Columbia 20231

Disclosure of _____
Your Name(s)

Entitled: _____
Title of Disclosure

Sir:

Attached is a copy of a disclosure of my above-entitled invention (consisting of _____ sheets of written description and _____ separate drawings or photos), a $_____ check and a stamped receipt postcard.

The undersigned respectfully requests that this disclosure be accepted and retained for two years (or longer if it is later referred to in a paper filed in a patent application) under the Disclosure Document Program and that the enclosed postcard be date stamped, numbered and returned.

The undersigned understands that (1) this disclosure document is neither a patent application nor a substitute for one, (2) its receipt date will not become the effective filing date of a later-filed patent application, (3) it will be retained for two years and then destroyed unless it is referred to in a patent application, (4) this two-year retention period is not a "grace period" during which a patent application can be filed without loss of benefits, (5) in addition to this document, proof of diligence in building and testing the invention, and/or filing a patent application on the invention, may be vital in case of an interference, and in other situations, (6) if such building and testing is done, signed, and dated, records of such should additionally be made and these should be witnessed and dated by disinterested individuals (not the PTO), and (7) if any public use or sale of the invention is made in the U.S., or any publication is made anywhere, no valid patent can be granted on the invention unless a patent application is filed on it within one year of any such public use, sale or publication, regardless of the filing date of this Disclosure Document.

Very respectfully,

_____   _____
Signature of Inventor   Signature of Joint Inventor

_____   _____
c/o (Print Name)   Print Name

_____   _____
Address   Address

_____   _____

Enclosures:
As stated above

Invention Disclosure

Sheet _____ of _____

Inventor(s): _____

Address(es): _____

Title of Invention: _____

To record **Conception**, describe: 1. Circumstances of conception, 2. Purposes and advantages of invention, 3. Description, 4. Sketches, 5. Operation, 6. Ramifications, 7. Possible novel features, and 8. Closest known prior art. To record **Building and Testing**, describe: 1. Any previous disclosure of conception, 2. Construction, 3. Ramifications, 4. Operation and Tests, and 5. Test results. Include sketches and photos, where possible. Continue on additional identical copies of this sheet if necessary; inventors and witnesses should sign all sheets.

Inventor(s): _____ Date: _____

_____ Date: _____

The above confidential information is Witnessed and Understood:

_____ Date: _____

_____ Date: _____

Provisional Patent Application Cover Letter

In the United States Patent and Trademark Office

Box Provisional Patent Application   Mailed 200 _____

Assistant Commissioner for Patents

Washington, District of Columbia 20231

Sir:

Please file the enclosed Provisional Patent Application (PPA) papers listed below under 37 C.F.R. § 1.53(b)(2).

Each of the undersigned understands:

A. This PPA is not a substitute for a Regular Patent Application (RPA), cannot be converted to an RPA, cannot get into interference with an RPA of another person, cannot be amended, will not be published, cannot claim any foreign priority, and will not mature into a patent;

B. If an RPA referring to this PPA is not filed within one year of the filing date of this PPA, this PPA will be worthless and will be destroyed;

C. Any desired foreign Convention applications (including PCT applications) based upon this PPA *must* be filed within one year of the filing date of this PPA;

D. This PPA *must* contain a written description of the invention, and of the manner and process of making and using it, in such full, clear, concise, and exact terms as to enable any person skilled in the art to which it pertains, or with which it is most nearly connected, to make and use the same, and shall set forth the best mode contemplated by the inventor of carrying out his invention. 35 U.S.C. § 112, ¶ 1. Otherwise this PPA will be worthless.

E. Any RPA will be entitled to claim the benefit of this PPA only if such RPA names at least one inventor of this PPA and this PPA discloses such inventor's invention, as claimed in at least one claim of the RPA, in the matter provided in Item D above.

Tentative Applicant # 1, Name: _____

Tentative Applicant # 2, Name: _____

Title: _____

(   ) Specification, sheets: _____   (   ) Drawing(s), sheets : _____

(   ) Check for $ _____   for   (   ) small entity   (   ) large entity filing fee

(   ) Return Receipt Postcard Addressed to Applicant # 1.

Very respectfully,

_____   _____

Applicant # 1 Signature   Applicant # 2 Signature

_____   _____

Address (Send Correspondence Here)   Address

_____   _____

Express Mail Label # (   ) ;   **Date of Deposit 200 ___**

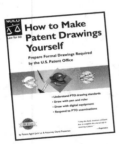

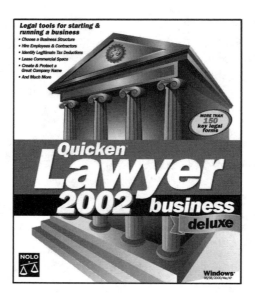

INVOICE

NOLO

950 Parker St.
Berkeley, CA 94710-2524
Phone: 510-549-1976
Fax: 510-548-5902
FEIN: 94-2759757

Page	Customer ID	Invoice ID
1	963697	**1097078**

Order Date
12/6/2004

Sold To:

Javier Hernandez
80 Descanso Dr. 3112
San Jose, CA 95134

Ship To:

Javier Hernandez
80 Descanso Dr. 3112
San Jose, CA 95134

Ship To ID: 963697

Customer PO#	Payment By	Rep	Shipped Via	Terms	Ordered By
	Discover		UPS Ground Res.		

ISBN	Title	List Price	Ordered	Ship	Back Order	Disc	Net	Extension
0-87337-599-8	Inventor's Notebook INOT3	19.99	1	1			19.99	19.99

1.28   Total Units Shipped: 1

Product Total	Sales Tax	Shipping	Invoice Total	Pre-Paid	Paid With Order	Balance Due
$19.99	$1.65	$5.00	$26.64	$0.00	$26.64	$0.00

NOLO

Registration Card

NAME _____ DATE _____

ADDRESS _____

_____

CITY _____ STATE _____ ZIP _____

PHONE _____ E-MAIL _____

WHERE DID YOU HEAR ABOUT THIS PRODUCT? _____

WHERE DID YOU PURCHASE THIS PRODUCT? _____

DID YOU CONSULT A LAWYER? (PLEASE CIRCLE ONE)   YES   NO   NOT APPLICABLE

DID YOU FIND THIS BOOK HELPFUL?   (VERY)   5   4   3   2   1   (NOT AT ALL)

COMMENTS _____

_____

_____

WAS IT EASY TO USE?   (VERY EASY)   5   4   3   2   1   (VERY DIFFICULT)

INOT 3.2

Nolo *in the* NEWS

"Nolo helps lay people perform legal tasks without the aid—or fees—of lawyers."

—USA TODAY

Nolo books are ..."written in plain language, free of legal mumbo jumbo, and spiced with witty personal observations."

—ASSOCIATED PRESS

"...Nolo publications...guide people simply through the how, when, where and why of law."

—WASHINGTON POST

"Increasingly, people who are not lawyers are performing tasks usually regarded as legal work... And consumers, using books like Nolo's, do routine legal work themselves."

—NEW YORK TIMES

"...All of [Nolo's] books are easy-to-understand, are updated regularly, provide pull-out forms...and are often quite moving in their sense of compassion for the struggles of the lay reader."

—SAN FRANCISCO CHRONICLE

- - - - - - - - - - - - - - - - - - fold here - - - - - - - - - - - - - - - - - -

Place
stamp here

Nolo
950 Parker Street
Berkeley, CA 94710-9867

Attn: INOT 3.2